Leadership By Serving

Mickey L. Burnim

Copyright © 2024 Mickey L. Burnim

Cover Art Copyright © 2024 Debbie O'Byrne

Book design by JETLAUNCH

ISBN: 979-8-89079-089-7 (Paperback)
ISBN: 979-8-89079-090-3 (Ebook)

Published by Mickey L. Burnim

All rights reserved.

No part of this publication may be reproduced, stored in a retrieval system, or transmitted in any form or by any means, electronic, mechanical, photocopying, recording, scanning, or otherwise, without prior written consent by the author.

TABLE OF CONTENTS

Acknowledgements v
Foreword vii
Prologue xi

Chapter 1: My Early Years 1
    Introduction 1
    My Waco Summer Experience 6
    Desegregating Teague High School. 12
    My Undergraduate Experience 16
Chapter 2: Pursuing the PhD .20
Chapter 3: From Scholar to Administrator. 27
Chapter 4: Learning About Leadership 35
    Learning About Leadership at NCCU 40
    The Search for a New Leader 49
    Working with the New Chancellor. 52
    Building the Leadership Team 60
    Establishing a Shared Vision 66
    Senator Basnight 74
    The Leadership Development Institute. 78
    Case: "A Disgruntled Worker?" 84

A Leadership Dilemma 87
Books: To Rent or Buy? 90
    The Board Meeting 93
Between a Rock and a Hard Place 96
The BSU Interview Process 109
Meeting the Chancellor 113
The Campus Visit 115
Meeting with the Board .123
New Opportunities, New Challenges 124
A New Provost 135
The Second New Provost .139
The Third New Provost 153
Leading the CIAA 156
The Commencement Venue 175
Service under Grace 187
Moving Forward 194
Notes 197

ACKNOWLEDGEMENTS

This is a book about leadership as told through stories taken from my forty-plus-year career in higher education. The stories are related as I remember them, and the people and places are real except for a few instances where I changed names and descriptions to protect people's privacy. Because of the passage of time, some of the dialogue has been recreated to reflect the meaning and tone as I recall them. Knowing that no book is perfect, I accept full responsibility for remaining errors, and deny any malevolent intent.

I am indebted to many people for their assistance in completing this book. These include my extraordinarily supportive wife and life partner, LaVera Levels Burnim; my memoir writing teacher, Cathy Smith, and my fellow students in her classes; Cathy Cruise, my editor; Dr. Jeanette Hawkins Evans, Dr. Ian Strachan, Dr. William Pollard, Dr. Mellonee Burnim, Dr. Freeman Hrabowski, and Walter Huntley, Jr. who read and commented on various drafts; Walter Davenport, Charles Penny, and Dr. Derrick Wilkins, all of whom helped me with remembering and researching; and Cinnamon Bowser who assisted me with social media.

Finally, I would be remiss without acknowledging the influence and impact of countless men and women who helped, in one way or another, to create the stories that I share in this volume. I am the product of all that I have seen and heard and experienced. Hence, they all deserve some credit, or blame, for who I am and, therefore, for these stories. Above all, I thank my God who continues to love, guide, protect, and forgive me. To Him be the glory for all He has done!

FOREWORD

When the great educator Mary Bethune launched her academy for girls of color in 1904, she began with a philosophy based on lessons learned from her teacher, Lucy Laney, the founder of the Haines Institute. Bethune truly believed that great teachers show students how to be lifelong seekers of knowledge. Bethune's school, which started as the Daytona Literary and Industrial Training School for Negro Girls, and eventually became Bethune-Cookman University, had humble beginnings. In the early years, students used squished elderberries as ink, charcoal wood for chalk, and dry good boxes for desks. When a potential donor, Mr. Gamble of Proctor and Gamble, visited her there, he asked, "Where is this school?" She replied, "In my mind and in my soul."

Mickey Burnim, the son of teachers who began their careers four decades after Bethune, was reared in a home and community that gave him the nurturing and self confidence that led to his becoming a leader at a young age. In fact, Burnim has been a lifelong student of leadership. This book recounts his journey, including his education and his professional career.

What makes the journey so interesting is his honesty, not only about his moments of joy, but also about his failures and disappointments. For example, at the beginning of the book he surprises the reader with a suspenseful moment involving his having failed the comprehensive doctoral examination in economics twice—an experience to which a number of graduate students can relate. We see this leader as a human being displaying vulnerability in a way that leaders rarely do. His willingness to be vulnerable shows us the source of his success—his humility and his faith in humanity and in God. He is comfortable talking about both.

We are living in a society in which leaders are attacked every day. We are watching Congress, the media and social media demean leaders—even Ivy League University Presidents—as never before. Right now, more than 20 HBCU presidencies are vacant. We hear regularly about declining enrollments, votes of no confidence, board conflicts, political intrusion, and student protests. The question becomes, why would someone want to become a college president, and what does it take to succeed in this position? Many educators are wanting as much information as possible about people who have had successful presidencies. Unfortunately, many well-meaning, hard-working educators leave presidencies under a cloud. Burnim was fortunate to have had long and successful presidencies at two institutions. Here are several of the essential lessons he distills from his experiences:

- Learning to manage upward, even when your boss is a micro manager,
- Learning how to deal with powerful politicians,
- Dealing with disloyal staff members,
- Balancing personal priorities against professional challenges,
- Appreciating support from family,
- Learning from your mistakes, and

- Honing your skills to evaluate people when hiring (always talking to the immediate supervisor of the candidate you plan to hire).

Burnim's story is an inspiring saga about a man who is always determined to do the right thing—to put students first—and who, like Mary Bethune, always kept ethical leadership in his mind and in his soul.

Freeman Hrabowski

PROLOGUE

As I sat there on the grassy hillside holding the unopened envelope in my hand, I felt more afraid than I had ever been in my life. No one else was around on this early fall afternoon and I felt alone with nature, isolated and very small in a vast universe. The envelope contained the results of my PhD preliminary examination—a very high-stakes test that would determine whether I would be allowed to continue in my graduate program or be summarily dismissed. I had already taken it twice . . . and failed it twice. *This is absolutely my last chance,* I thought. *If I fail again, what am I going to do? How will I support my family? What kind of career path will I then have? How did I get to this point? Oh, God, what must I do?* I asked myself these penetrating questions as I held the unopened envelope in my hand.

I, and the forty or so other students who took the examination, had been waiting three weeks for the results. I'd gotten little rest during those weeks and could think of nothing else. At this point, I had already invested three years of my life in this program, pursuing my dream of becoming a professor of economics and following that path to personal fulfillment while caring for my wife, LaVera, and our five-year old daughter, Cinnamon. Our son, Adrian, would come years later.

LaVera's investment had been considerable also. She agreed to move with me from her family in Texas so that I could enroll in the University of Wisconsin Madison graduate program. And she did so even though she was very close to her family and some of them did not understand why this sacrifice made sense. When we told her father that we were moving to Wisconsin so I could work on a doctorate in economics, he asked, "Are there graduate programs in Texas where you can study that?"

"Yes sir, there are, but the Wisconsin program has a philosophical bent that is more aligned with the degree I received at North Texas and with my personal preferences." This was my best effort to convince him that it made sense. As he stood in front of me, slowly nodding his head up and down and saying, "I see," I had the uneasy feeling that he was not convinced.

LaVera had also made a career sacrifice. With her newly minted bachelor of business administration degree in accounting, she left the opportunities of working with Big Eight accounting firms in Dallas or Houston to travel with me to Madison, Wisconsin, and settle for an entry-level government auditing position.

Finally, there was tremendous personal shame at stake. I had enrolled in this graduate program with some arrogance. I came with a master's degree and had always been successful. I was a very disciplined person and was always willing to work as hard as was needed to achieve my goals. If I had failed the exam again, how would it affect my relationship with my wife? I knew that she loved me but wondered how this sad chapter might somehow cause her to see me as less than the man she thought she had married. What would my professors from my baccalaureate and master's degree programs think? They had been so proud to send one of their prize students off to a top graduate program. Then there was the race factor. I was the only African American in my entering cohort of forty-five students. If I failed, it would not just be personal, but it would feed the racist view that Blacks just couldn't cut it in a rigorous graduate program.

What follows are stories showing how I got to this point in my life, and then moved beyond it to be a servant leader in several leadership opportunities.

1

MY EARLY YEARS

INTRODUCTION

I was a five-year-old first grader at Furney Richardson School this bright and warm fall morning. Miss Bluitt, my first-grade teacher, was teaching us about the danger of fire and how we should always be careful with matches. She was a tall, ample woman who taught us while sitting behind her desk at the front of the classroom. The blackboard covered the front wall behind her. I was already listening for the recess bell that would sound soon, but I was still present enough to be one of the first students to raise my hand to answer her question, "Why are matches dangerous?"

"You might get burned or burn your house down," I replied proudly.

Recess was a favorite part of the day for me because I loved running around the school yard playing hide-and-seek or dodge ball, or swinging in the sturdy, high-flying swing set on the playground for elementary students. Furney Richardson School had three buildings, which accommodated classes from the first through the twelfth grade. The building for the elementary classes sat about a hundred yards back from the paved two-lane farm-to-market road that was the southern border of the school yard. Closer to the road and right of the elementary building was the high school building, which actually included classrooms for seventh through twelfth grades. The third building was to the left of ours and it was where home economics, agriculture, and shop classes were taught. The four swings and a dirt basketball court were in the center of the campus. A wire fence stood a few feet from the road along the school property to protect students from automobile traffic.

When the recess bell rang, all the children in the building ran out of their classrooms for a fifteen-minute break from our schoolwork and some fun! First, we ran to the outhouse to relieve ourselves. In the mid-1950s, this rural, segregated school had no indoor restrooms, so we went to the wooden whitewashed structure that was our outdoor restroom. One side was marked "Boys" and the other side "Girls."

As we were leaving the outhouse, I noticed a couple of large concrete blocks and had an idea! "Hey guys," I said to two or three of my classmates, "I bet those blocks would be good for striking matches." I don't remember where I got them, but I produced some matches and we had great fun dragging the match heads across the porous and rough concrete surfaces. We were behind the classroom buildings and a hundred yards or so from our building, so I didn't think there was much chance Miss Bluitt would see us. I was mistaken.

As soon as we returned to her classroom after recess, Miss Bluitt called me and the other boys to her desk at the front of the classroom. "Didn't we just talk about the danger of playing with matches and why you shouldn't do it?"

"Yes, ma'am."

"Hold out your hands." She then used her wooden paddle to reinforce that lesson and to incentivize us to do a better job of applying what we had learned in the future. Though it certainly was not an example of good leadership, it illustrates my propensity for leading. As far back as I can remember,

I was selected for, elected to, or volunteered for leadership positions.

It helped a great deal that I was blessed to be in a supportive and nurturing ecosystem composed of my parents, teachers, church members, and coaches who believed in me and encouraged me, and when necessary, corrected me. All of this support helped me to develop a strong reservoir of self-confidence, which is an essential aspect of effective leadership.

It started, of course, with my parents, who reared my sisters, Mellonee and Wonda, and myself in a loving, nurturing, and comfortable middle-class home. Dad had an outsized personality that owed, in part, to his six-feet-three-inch frame and commanding voice, though he was not boisterous. He had an outgoing personality and a generous spirit. He was the agriculture teacher at the Furney Richardson School and very active in that community. He loved assisting the Black farmers in the area when they had a cow struggling with a difficult delivery of a calf, or a litter of pigs that needed vaccinations, or chickens that needed antibiotics. Throughout his career, he also loved encouraging students, whether his or not, to go to college, and was eager to help them do so.

Sometimes he would personally advocate for students who had special talents. One such student was Marvin Levels, one of his outstanding high school basketball players whose younger sister I would marry some years later. Dad called several college coaches to encourage them to recruit Marvin, who was a solid student, a fine young man, and superb basketball player. This was 1965 and some of the walls of segregation were starting to come down a little, but not nearly enough. Marvin accepted a scholarship to a junior college and later transferred to Harding College in Arkansas where he had a great career, graduated, and went on to become a teacher and coach himself.

Mom was also tall for a woman of her generation, standing five feet, seven inches tall. Where Dad's personality was a bit oversized because of his height and his voice, Mom was soft-spoken and deferential. She had a sweet spirit about her and was respectful of everyone that she encountered.

Dad and Mom met at Prairie View A&M College where he studied agriculture and mom majored in home economics. They both had been raised on subsistence family farms in rural East Texas and had arrived at Prairie View only with encouraging and supportive assistance from close family and friends.

One day shortly after his high school graduation, Dad was chopping wood on the family farm outside Nacogdoches when someone delivered a telegram to him that said: "Arzo, I've managed to get a job for you at Prairie View so you can work your way through college! Get down to Prairie View as soon as you can." It was sent by one of his high school teachers who had recognized his potential. His father, my grandfather, sold a cow to get money to buy a bus ticket and sent Dad on his way. Once there, he worked in the campus laundry to pay his tuition, fees, and living expenses. Thus, Dad became the first in his family to go to college and so laid out a vision of possibilities and a path for his siblings and his own children to come.

It was Mom's mother who played a key role in getting her to Prairie View. Grandmother Leola convinced Daddy Joe to send Mom to college. Even though he had spent a year at Prairie View himself and Mom's older sister had gone to college, he had never considered that path for Mom. "What? Dell wants to go to college?" was how Mom described his initial reaction to the idea. In telling the story years later, Mom suggested that her less-than-distinguished high school record may have colored his opinion. Nevertheless, they sent her to Prairie View where she attended college with her precocious twin cousins, Ruth and Ramona. Mom worked in the campus dining hall to help pay her school expenses.

They both graduated in 1947 and began their teaching careers in the segregated public schools of Texas. Dad started out teaching agriculture in the Furney Richardson School three miles in the country outside Teague, and Mom began teaching home economics back at home in the Black township of Neylandville, which was just outside Greenville. They married in December of that year and Mom left her teaching job to join Dad in Furney Richardson. She then devoted her life to making a home and rearing her children, returning to teaching only after my youngest sister, Wonda, was old enough to go to school with her. Dad served the traditional breadwinner role by teaching and coaching in segregated public schools. Together they ensured that we had enriching experiences, including piano lessons for my sisters, cub scouts for me, and band participation for all of us, as well as rich church experiences like Sunday school, and Christmas and Easter programs. In addition, Mom and Dad constantly told us that we could become anything we wanted to, and expressed their high expectations for us. Their loving, nurturing upbringing gave my sisters and me a firm faith foundation, encouragement to not let others limit us, and self-confidence to lead others with humility.

I also benefited from broader community encouragement and support from teachers, community church leaders, and relatives. Miss Bluitt was one example, but there were many others, including Miss Clewis, who taught me the proper fingering for the QWERTY keyboard that was the standard for typewriters. This still serves me well today as I write with my computer keyboard. There were also Mr. Gillespie, who was my football coach, Ms. Reese, who taught me grammar, composition, and literature and held high expectations for us, and Mr. Snipes, who taught me parliamentary procedure and coached me as a member of the tennis team.

By the time I reached the fourth grade, Dad had taken a job in Teague at the combined J. A. Brooks Elementary/ Booker T. Washington High schools. That year, in Ms. Jordan's class, I was elected class president and, as memory serves, was subsequently voted either class president or vice president for my class throughout the rest of my public school career. These dedicated men and women afforded me many opportunities to develop leadership skills and build confidence. I participated in a chapter conducting competition using Robert's Rules of Order, showed my Yorkshire pig in 4-H competitions, and competed in district and state-level interscholastic league and band competitions. These leadership-developing opportunities even extended to my high school sports participation. I played doubles on the tennis team and quarterback on the football team, and was eventually selected to be one of the team captains.

I recall that during one of our evening practices for an upcoming game, I was presumptuous enough to suggest some new plays to the coach for us to use. "Coach, I saw the LA Rams run this spread formation on Sunday," I said, "and I think it would work well for us by allowing us to use both our quarterbacks on the same play!" After seeing my diagrams of the plays, the coach actually added them to our playbook! My leadership opportunities also extended beyond the primary and secondary schools. In Sunday school, I was sometimes given the chance to teach the lesson to my class, and was often selected to give the lesson review when all the classes assembled to share what they had learned.

My Waco Summer Experience

My propensity toward leading was subtly, but definitely, boosted by the freedom given and sacrifices made by my parents. Their decisions to trust me and allow me to take calculated risks served as powerful encouragement and reinforcement of my leadership tendencies. Beyond simple provision, their parenting was key. A poignant illustration of their support is how they allowed me to use the family car for some personal enrichment opportunities during the summer before my senior year of high school. I had read in the *Waco Morning Herald* about a slide rule class for high school students being offered at Baylor University and thought that was a good skill to have, as I prepared to start college in another year. The slide rule was a calculation tool for crunching large numbers that predated the electronic handheld calculator. I didn't have a particular need to know how to use a slide rule at the time, but I figured that it might come in handy in the future, as I had seen students at Prairie View A&M University walking the campus with slide rules dangling from their belts. "Dad, can I sign up and take this class at Baylor this summer?" I asked. "Mr. Moore will be driving there every day for his graduate course and I could ride with him." I hadn't given much thought to the fact that this was 1965 and desegregation was still a dirty word across much of the South, including our region of central Texas. In all likelihood, Dad was well aware that if I went, I would probably be the only African American student in the class. In spite of that, Dad gave his consent, and even offered to let me drive our car some of the time and share the burden with Mr. Moore. He was trusting a sixteen-year-old to drive the family car more than fifty miles one way to a much larger city, where I would have to negotiate heavier traffic in an unfamiliar, if not outright hostile, environment. Of course, I would be commuting with Mr. Moore, who was a teacher and could be expected to be a moderating influence on any immature adolescent temptations. That Dad would allow me to go despite possible resistance probably reflected some of his personal rebellion against racism as well as his belief that I would not be facing any real physical danger.

Mr. Moore was the music teacher at my high school, as well as a good family friend. We became across-the-street neighbors on West 5th Avenue in Teague when, in 1956, we rented a house almost directly opposite where he lived with his grandmother. "E. V.," as he was known then, was small in stature, about five foot five, but he possessed enormous musical talent and was known widely throughout the region as a music prodigy. He was in great demand to play piano for church choirs and soloists near and far. His musical talent extended to the alto saxophone, and we played in the high school band together when he was a senior and I was in sixth grade.

E. V. graduated from Booker T. Washington High School and went to Wiley College, an historically Black college (HBCU) in Marshall, Texas, where he majored in music. After graduation from Wiley, he returned to Booker T. as the music teacher and was then referred to by students and teachers alike as "Mr. Moore." This was both a reflection of the great esteem that African Americans held for their teachers and the formality with which African Americans in the South interacted.

Though it did cover some fifty-two miles, the drive from Teague to Waco was along a straight two-lane highway through acres and acres of flat farmland and pastures, except for passing through Mexia (pronounced Ma-hair). Mexia, then, was a town of about 6,000 people, twelve miles west of Teague, my hometown. Being more than twice the size of Teague, driving through it was like sampling a visual buffet of life in a larger town. Slowing to comply with the thirty-mile-per-hour speed limit in Mexia, we passed many gas stations, H-E-B and Brookshire grocery stores, a Dairy Queen hamburger joint with a separate service window for "Colored" patrons on the side of the building, and several "Whites Only" cafes and restaurants. The commute went by quickly, as Mr. Moore and I had lively conversations about whatever crossed our minds. He would often tell me about discussions from his Baylor graduate course, which involved the dissection and analysis of Gilbert and Sullivan's opera, *The Mikado*. I could tell from the excitement in his voice that he found the subject matter interesting and enjoyed the challenge of the discussions with his classmates and teacher.

My slide rule classes passed without incident. There was nothing glitzy about them, just the essential bare bones of how to use a slide rule. The inexpensive one I purchased in the Baylor University book store served me well for participating in the class and learning the fundamentals of its use. I don't recall if there were any other students of color in the class, but the mere fact that I remember so little about the class tells me that all went smoothly. The next year, I actually found a use for my new tool and knowledge in my high school physics class. But after that, my slide rule quickly became my personal relic of a fast-receding era. This fascinating device, which had been invented in the 1600s, was already beginning its rapid descent into oblivion. The Hewlett-Packard Company was already developing the pocket calculator, which would be faster, more powerful, and easier to use than the slide rule. They would introduce it to the world just three years later in 1968.

As the end of the slide rule class approached, I saw another announcement in the *Waco Morning Herald* about a tennis camp at the Sul Ross Tennis Center. I had played doubles on my Booker T. Washington High School tennis team for two years, but had only been taught the game by our coach, Mr. Snipes, an agriculture teacher who had never had any formal tennis instruction himself. *Wow*, I thought, *how neat it would be to learn from a real tennis pro and really develop my skills!* In the back of my mind, I suspected that this public invitation to a tennis camp might not have been intended for Black teenagers like me, but it didn't matter. I wanted to participate and a public announcement and invitation had been issued in the daily newspaper.

Dad and Mom once again approved my plan, since I was already commuting with Mr. Moore and they could see the potential benefit of my participating in the camp. On the first day of the camp, it was Mr. Moore's turn to drive. He stopped the car in front of the tennis center. "I'll wait for you to get registered before driving on to my class," he offered. I walked into the tennis center pro shop dressed in my tennis whites and carrying my Wilson Jack Kramer Autograph wooden racquet under my arm. The pro shop was alive with activity as several White teenagers, dressed in their tennis gear, were about, some executing their assigned duties as employees of the center and others just hanging out. As I approached the front desk, I felt that all eyes were on me as Charlie McCleary, the director, greeted me with a quizzical look.

"Can I help you?" he asked.

"Yes, you can. I want to register for the tennis camp that was advertised in the newspaper."

McCleary responded with, "I think someone is teaching tennis over at A. J. Moore High School."

I wasn't sure, but I suspected he was trying to refer me to a Black high school in the city. There it was—a stark reminder that we were in the South and segregation was very much the expected social order. Truth be told, I was not entirely surprised by this attempted rebuff, and felt a controlled determination rising inside me. I said in a measured tone, "That's fine, but I want to sign up for the one here. I'm commuting with someone and it is very convenient. I know nothing about Moore High School, its tennis facilities, or its tennis instruction." It was not my manner to show a lot of emotion or to speak or act impulsively, but I was determined to be firm in what I wanted and to make my case clearly and logically.

McCleary retreated into an inner office, apparently to make a telephone call. The hum of activity in the Pro Shop continued, but I was sure that they had all heard the exchange and were listening carefully to see what the outcome would be. I knew that McCleary could have been calling the police, but suspected that he was seeking advice about how to deal with this situation from someone he reported to or trusted. After a few minutes, McCleary returned with the paperwork for me to register. I then waved to Mr. Moore and he drove on to his class.

Though it did turn out that there were no other boys of color at the tennis camp, the experience was a very positive one for me. Some of the detail has faded from memory, but I recall that there were sixteen hard courts in pristine condition with no cracks or irregularities in their surfaces, and nets that were strung precisely at regulation height, all very different from the outdoor courts that I had played on in the past. There were also aluminum bleachers for spectators, and even a pro shop for stringing racquets and selling tennis balls and accessories. As one of about out of fifty or so players in the camp, I learned a lot about tennis fundamentals and strategy, made a few friends, and experienced some good camaraderie with some of the regulars who taught in the camp and who spent a lot of time around the tennis center. After the scheduled camp sessions each day, I played and practiced with some of them. These after-camp practice sessions gave me a chance to hone the skills I had been taught in camp. We got along well together and enjoyed the friendly competition.

The final camp activity was a tournament featuring all of the participants, and I felt so proud because mom and dad had come to see me play in it. I introduced my parents to some of my new tennis friends and was pleasantly surprised when these White teenage boys greeted them as Mr. and Ms. Burnim! It was the first time that I had heard White males of any age address my parents by anything other than their first or last name with no honorific title. Those summer experiences in Waco had been positive for me in more ways than one, but probably most importantly, they were a huge boost to my ego and self-confidence!

Desegregating Teague High School

The beginning of school that fall was memorable for reasons beyond the fact that I entered it with significantly greater tennis prowess! The August 19, 1965, edition of the *Teague Chronicle,* our hometown newspaper, announced, "Members of the Board of Trustees of the Teague Independent School District have unanimously voted to abolish the 12th grade at Booker T. Washington High School and integrate the 32 seniors from the Negro school with Teague High School."[1] I was very excited by that news! Even though it had been a full eleven years since the US Supreme Court handed down the Brown v. Board of Education decision outlawing segregation in the public schools, change was finally coming to Teague, Texas! Additionally, this was two years after the 1963 Civil Rights March on Washington, and a year after the Civil Rights Act of 1964 was passed and signed into law, so I saw this change as being a big tangible connection to important happenings in our country! This was my first real chance to have an active part in the movement. I would show White teachers and students that Black students could be outstanding scholars and people. (I was only sixteen years old and quite naïve about the underlying causes of racism in America.)

Teague, located in central Texas, exhibited many of the characteristics of small towns across the South. Teague was bisected by the Burlington-Rock Island Railroad; Whites lived on one side on the railroad tracks and Blacks on the other. Main Street was on the White side of the tracks and lining it were the grocery stores, the post office, the doctor's office, drugstores, clothing and furniture stores, and other commercial enterprises—all of them White-owned and -operated. All of the streets on this side were paved. On the Black side of the tracks, virtually none of the streets were paved. Some were covered with red gravel, but many were simply made of dirt that had been smoothed over by a big Caterpillar road grader. Commerce on that side of town consisted of a beauty shop and one or two barbershops, a small corner convenience store, and sometimes a cafe that had a loud jukebox and sold plates of fried fish.

Hence, the desegregation of the senior class was a big deal to me—an opportunity to show White people that Black people were not inherently inferior as suggested by the racist messages that pervaded our society. We would be able to compete head-to-head academically and athletically, and, in so doing, make our contribution to the Civil Rights Movement! (Ahh, the optimism of youth!)

The Teague Chronicle was published on Thursdays, so when Dad arrived home Friday evening from a week of summer school at Prairie View A&M University, the big news about the school board decision was still very fresh. I barely allowed him to get in the house before I blurted out, "Dad, the school board voted to integrate the public schools by sending the senior class at Booker T. to Teague High School, and you and Mr. Moore were also reassigned to teach there!" As the news sank in, I could see Dad's pleasant homecoming smile change to a worried frown. This puzzled me, because I had expected Dad to be excited like I was. But his body language was showing distress. Some years later, I came to appreciate how his having grown up in rural East Texas in the 1930s, where race relations were notoriously bad, had provided the context for his interpretation of this news of sudden school desegregation. He had seen extreme racism up close and personal, and he knew that the Black students and teachers would be under a dangerous microscope at Teague High School. In spite of this, he and Mr. Moore accepted their new assignments and made the transition.

One day during the first week of school, the senior class held a meeting to elect class officers. One of my Black classmates nominated me to be president, and several of the White students nominated one of our White classmates. When the vote was taken, the White students split their votes among the several White candidates and the Black students voted in a block for me. One of the White nominees voted for me and I, in turn, voted for him. I saw those votes as goodwill gestures attempting to create a unifying effect. Our fathers were quail hunting buddies and, years earlier, on occasion, Mom took me and my sister with her when she was hired to babysit him and his brothers; so we had known each other for years. I was elected class president for the first desegregated class in the Teague Independent School District! I was pleased, and it was big news. *The Dallas Morning News* even sent a reporter to interview me and the story was actually printed.

When spring sports started up during my senior year at the newly desegregated Teague High School, I tried out for the tennis team along with several other boys. During the previous two years at Booker T. Washington, my tennis specialty had been doubles. I loved the teamwork and coordination that doubles required. The court positioning and game tactics made the competition somewhat akin to a chess match. I would serve the ball to a spot that limited the opponent's return options, and my partner would anticipate the return shot and put it away for a winner!

However, during senior-year tryouts, my summer camp-enhanced skills and knowledge of the game enabled me to establish myself as the best individual player, and so the coach declared that I would play the number one singles position. I played this position for the first match of my senior season and managed, with some struggle, to win it. Playing good singles requires one to be in excellent physical condition, and I was not there. Unlike doubles, when playing singles, I had no partner to rely on for help! That first singles match forced me to play at the limits of my conditioning to get the win and, afterwards, I declared, "I am done with singles; it's too hard! Doubles is my game!" When the coach overheard me complain about the rigors of singles, she expressed her disappointment that I would give up so easily. I didn't like the idea of being labeled a quitter and thought, "Well, if I'm going to play singles, I have to get in better shape." The next week, I started getting out of bed an hour earlier and going for a conditioning run before school every day!

After a couple of weeks of this regimen, my improved conditioning allowed me to be a more formidable competitor. I won a number of matches during the season and advanced to the finals in our high school district tournament, which was played at the same Sul Ross Tennis Center where I had attended camp! So some of the friends that I had made there the previous summer were able to watch me play in the district tournament. It felt really good to have my own fan club, even though this predated the very vocal cheering and jeering that is so common in tennis today. I didn't fully appreciate it at the time, but in retrospect, I can see that my parents placed a lot of confidence in me as a teenager. Even though I lost that match, my summer experience in Waco had been a powerful boost to my personal confidence, which later proved to be a critical factor in my various leadership roles.

Growing up in a supportive and nurturing community, even within a larger racist society, was a real advantage for me. I benefited from the encouragement and high expectations of my parents, teachers, and other Black adult leaders. Encouragement and support can be powerful assets in anyone's life, and I am convinced that those who can give this to others are obligated to do so!

My Undergraduate Experience

When time came to choose a college to continue my education, I decided to attend North Texas State University in spite of the fact that both of my parents had graduated from Prairie View A&M University and I had grown up planning to go there also. Prairie View was the 1890 land grant HBCU in Texas, my parents were alumni, and that was where all of the statewide athletic and academic competitions culminated. Texas, like the rest of the South, was still operating largely in a postsecondary educational environment of de facto segregation. "Going to state" in football, basketball, track, or interscholastic league competition (music, drama, numbers sense, spelling, typing, etc.) meant earning a trip to Prairie View in pursuit of a state championship! For many reasons, Prairie View was embedded in my psyche, and throughout my first three years of high school, I had planned to go there.

But the mid-1960s was the height of the Civil Rights Movement and a lot of traditional barriers were being challenged. Hence, continuing in my naiveté about American racism, instead of going to my preferred HBCU, I chose to matriculate at a predominantly White university—North Texas State University—where I expected to excel and, in so doing, help move our society past the myth that White people were inherently superior to Black people.

In the fall of 1966, North Texas State University enrolled about 15,000 students, fewer than 1,000 of whom were African American. While the campus was clearly moving in the right direction by admitting Black students and even giving us the option of living in on-campus residence halls, it had the feel of being a campus for White students and lacked the adaptations necessary for ethnic diversity to thrive. There were no Black faculty or staff members, no accommodations for mitigating the social isolation inherent in those numbers, and no system for emotional support.

But even in this environment, I gravitated toward leadership positions. During my second semester, I ran for and was elected floor representative in my residence hall governance association. Part of my campaign strategy was to knock on every door of my floor and ask the residents to vote for me—and many did. In my sophomore year, I used that experience and exposure as a launching pad for a successful run for sophomore senator in the campus-wide Student Government Association—United Students of North Texas (USNT). My conscientious service as sophomore senator and ability to work and get along with others in the USNT provided a great stepping stone to my successful candidacy for junior class president the next year.

At this point, I had served in some type of elected position every semester after my very first one, and through my service activities and the notoriety that came from my name being frequently mentioned in the university newspaper, I had become widely known across campus. During my year of service as junior class president, some of the USNT officers encouraged me to run for USNT vice president for my senior year. The vice president presided over the Senate, which was the legislative branch of student government on which I had served. I acceded to the urgings to run, and was elected as the first Black student senate president. In *The Story of North Texas: From Texas Normal College, 1890, to the University of North Texas System, 2001*, author James L. Rogers reported, "He also was vice president of the student body, president of both the junior and senior classes, and one of the first

Black residents of West Hall, the first men's residence to be desegregated."² By this point in my life, I had become very comfortable with serving in leadership positions, and was learning that my methodical, conservative, and integrity-based approach could be very successful.

It was during my sophomore year at North Texas State that I made a decision that would set the course for my life's work. My freshman year at the university had been a wonderful overall experience. The academic environment and intellectual stimulation resonated with my soul, and made me feel that I was created to grow, develop, and thrive in such a place. I loved the challenges of my classes—being introduced to new facts and ideas; being taught history, public speaking, and the scientific method; and engaging in thoughtful discussion and debate. I felt a strong call to life in the academy. The image of sitting in a small faculty office overlooking the campus quadrangle and thinking deep thoughts about economic problems, solutions, and approaches really appealed to me. The thought of always being in close proximity to a great library so that I could research issues of interest to me whenever I wanted was simply exhilarating!

Hence, I marched into my department chair's office and announced, "Dr. Cochran: I want to be a professor of economics! What do I need to do?"

Cochran was very formal in his personal interactions and his tendency was to be direct. "Well, Mickey, you will need to spend several years in graduate school. What's your grade point average?"

I quickly answered, "2.75." This was just below a straight "B" average and one that had earned me quite a bit of recognition and respect among the other African American males on campus, since this placed me in the upper echelon of academic achievers from this group.

"Well, you need to get serious about your academic work and graduate with honors!" he retorted. "You should also take more mathematics courses, at least through calculus, to prepare for a graduate economics program."

Following Cochran's advice, I graduated with honors in three-and-a-half years. My enrollment in graduate school was delayed a bit because I got married and started a family and needed to work to support my family. After a year and a half, I quit my job and returned to NTSU to finish my master's degree in economics. During that year, I applied and was accepted into the economics graduate program at the University of Wisconsin-Madison, where I would study for the PhD, a necessary step to become a professor of economics.

2
PURSUING THE PHD

There were forty-five students in my entering cohort at Wisconsin. Many of them had graduated from universities in the Midwest and Northeast, including the University of Connecticut, American University, Cornell University, the University of Pennsylvania, and Michigan State, but this group also included rich representation from other states and several international programs. These included the University of New Zealand, the University of Georgia, and my own North Texas State University. The only other student of color was a fellow from North Africa—Ethiopia, I think. These were some of the best students from their respective universities and so the competition was inherently keen. The intensity of the graduate program and the sheer volume of required reading led us to form study groups, which facilitated our learning from each other. As I had expected, this economics graduate program was stretching me to my limits.

At the end of the first year, students were required to sit for a comprehensive examination in economic theory, and passing of this examination constituted official entry to the PhD program. It was a written examination of three to four hours in length, and it was based loosely, but not exclusively, on information taught in the courses taken that first year.

There was no fixed body of literature to study and master, but rather the whole of economic theory was fair game for the exam. For the most part, the questions did not have definitive fixed answers. Instead, two faculty members would read and grade each answer based on their knowledge and judgment. If their evaluations differed from each other markedly, a third faculty member read the answer and the evaluation of the first two. The one which most closely matched his became the final grade. I, like most of the students in my cohort, studied and prepared all summer for the examination, not knowing that this hurdle would prove to be the defining event for the rest of my life.

Departmental officials had told us to expect the results about three weeks after the examination. Individual test-takers would be notified via letters placed in their departmental mailboxes. Three weeks later, I gathered at the mailboxes along with other students who had gotten the word that the envelopes containing the results had been placed in our boxes. As expected, there was a lot of excitement in the air. I opened my letter and was dumbstruck to see "Fail" in the results space of the form letter! I had never failed anything before in my life! I had always been an exemplary student, always beginning work on assignments early and being assiduous in my preparation. When my intellectual giftedness was not enough, I made up for it by putting in more time and working harder. Failing this exam was quite embarrassing and a real blow to my ego. Not only that, but through my failure, I might actually be reinforcing the myth of racial inferiority, since I was the only African American in that cohort! In spite of all this, I was undeterred. I would petition to be allowed to take the following year's examination with the next cohort of students and would redouble my preparation activities.

My world had been rocked! I had to continue interacting with my cohort members by going to classes, working in study groups, and hanging out in the student offices, and do so by holding my head up and not let this failure define who I was. I would not let imagined conversations and whispers cause me to get down on myself. It really helped that LaVera was very patient and encouraging. "You can do this," she said. "You'll pass this exam."

By this time, LaVera and I were in our third year of marriage and had a two-year-old daughter. LaVera had made the tremendous sacrifice to move to Wisconsin with me so I could pursue this degree. She was not only far from her close knit family, but she had given up an amazing job opportunity as well. In light of these sacrifices, she had a right to feel some resentment at my failure. Instead, she lovingly smiled at me and declared, "You can pass exam."

That smile took me back to a spring afternoon in 1965 when our relationship had begun. She was standing on the front lawn of Booker T. Washington High School, holding a soft drink with both hands and sipping it through a straw. Her head was cocked slightly to one side and her face showed a faint smile. "What a pretty and interesting looking girl!" I thought. She would become my soulmate and the love of my life.

My petition was granted, and so the next summer I worked full-time preparing for the retake, even forgoing weekend breaks and days off with my wife and daughter. This meant eight hours a day for six and sometimes seven days a week of reading, working problems, reviewing and writing answers to questions from previous examinations. I was confident that I had the intellectual capacity to pass, and believed that working absolutely as hard as I could would get me over the hump. That exam would have to yield to my brute-strength approach!

When I sat for the examination that second time, I felt well prepared, but my confidence had been severely shaken from the experience of having failed it once. I attacked this version of the exam with vigor and some trepidation, turned it in, and then began what seemed like an interminable wait for the results. Three weeks later, the envelopes containing the results were placed in our mailboxes. This time, instead of opening the envelope immediately, I tucked it into my backpack and rode my bicycle along the lakeside path away from campus where I could be alone when I opened it. I turned off the path onto a hillside, got off my bike, and sat on the grass. As I unzipped my backpack to retrieve the letter, I could feel my heart beating inside my chest. Using my thumb as a letter opener, I separated the flap from the body of the envelope, took out the letter and unfolded it with slightly shaking hands. As I read it, I felt myself falling into the greatest depression I had ever experienced. I had failed the preliminary examination again! My dreams were disintegrating right before me! It was looking like my plan to become a university professor would not be realized! How would I support my family? I was letting down my wife and daughter and reinforcing the myth of racial inferiority! What would I do now?

As I sat there on the grass, I had to really fight to avoid being overcome by a penetrating fear. Would I be dismissed from the graduate program? If so, where would my family and I go? *Since Chicago was only 160 miles from Madison, perhaps I could go there and get a job as a stock broker*, I thought. *Or maybe I could get a job teaching economics in a community college rather than a university.*

After sitting with these thoughts for a few minutes, I had an epiphany! Though I had studied and prepared as hard and as completely as I knew how, I had still come up short. What was left? What were the next steps for me? What could I possibly do at this point? And in that moment, I knew! A small, still, inner voice spoke to me and said, "You can pray!"

I thought, *Wow! Where did that come from?* This thought was both surprising and revealing! Since my freshman year at North Texas State, I had claimed to be an agnostic. My freshman English teacher, Dr. Robert Stevens, had assigned our class to read an essay on the Holocaust. During the ensuing discussion, he declared, "I don't know if there is a God or not because, if there is, why would he allow six million Jews to be exterminated? So I am an agnostic." Even though I had been a Christian for almost ten years, as a very impressionable eighteen-year-old, I was persuaded by his logic and even extended it to the plight of Black people in America. I questioned, "If there really is a God, why would he allow millions of people to be abducted from Africa and brought through the horrible Middle Passage to be held in chattel slavery and brutalized for hundreds of years?" I didn't have an answer and hence decided that I, too, was an agnostic and, consequently, used this as a reason to challenge and disregard many of my long-held beliefs. I stopped praying and going to church and began engaging in a number of behaviors that were inconsistent with my Christian teachings and beliefs, such as striving harder to fit in with my peers by using vulgar language. So, for the thought "You can pray" to occur to me in that moment made me realize that I really did believe in an omniscient and omnipotent God—one who could give me answers and show me the way out of my bad situation! At that moment, I was moved to pray, "Lord, forgive me for doubting your goodness and wisdom. I acknowledge your omniscience and yield my situation to you." From then on, I joined my wife and daughter in going to church and endeavoring to be a sincere Christian disciple.

My path forward had suddenly become very uncertain. I didn't know what the future held for me but I was content to know that it was in God's hands. My faculty advisor said to me, "Mick, in this situation, I would normally advise you to find another doctoral program and get a fresh start, but you have a family and that would mean uprooting and disrupting their lives as well. Maybe the faculty will give you one more chance. I will be your advocate." The departmental decision-makers granted me a very rare third chance to take the theory preliminary examination. I would take it the following fall, three years after starting the program. In the meantime, I continued to take the required courses and began the process of preparing and writing a dissertation.

This time, the three-weeks wait felt just as long. I still didn't have an alternative career plan, but I didn't worry. I would either pass it or I wouldn't. I had prepared for the exam as well as I could and had given it my best. It was in God's hands.

I picked up my envelope and once again bicycled to my hillside spot. As before, I sat on the grass and opened my envelope. When I saw those capitalized block letters spelling out "PASS," I was as happy as one man could be! *"Hallelujah!"* Having gotten my attention, God had allowed me to overcome this hurdle and my career plan was back on track! Since I had continued to take classes and fulfill the other requirements, I went on to be one of the first five members of my cohort to defend my dissertation—the last requirement for the PhD.

In his letter of recommendation to aid me in getting a job, my faculty advisor wrote, "Mickey L. Burnim is one of the best-liked members of his cohort and, given the demands being placed on Black academics these days, I expect him to be a dean in five years and a president in fifteen years." This declaration planted a seed in my mind that one day I might become a university president. It turns out that his statement had a profound effect on me, just as one from my mother had when I was a young boy. She told me, "Mickey, you're going to be a great man!" I had no idea what she meant, but her statement was a powerful affirmation of my self-worth and contributed to my strong and positive self-image, and my tendency to hold high expectations for myself. I found my professor's observation to be interesting, but it didn't really phase me. My focus was on being a good faculty member and progressing by earning tenure and being promoted through the faculty ranks to professor.

3
FROM SCHOLAR TO ADMINISTRATOR

My first job after graduate school was as assistant professor at Florida State University in Tallahassee. I was really excited about it because the department offered bachelor's, master's, and doctoral degrees, and this meant that I would have the chance to teach students at all three of those levels. It also meant great opportunities for learning from and collaborating with colleagues who had active research projects and were busy publishing books and research papers. My appointment was also joint with the Institute for Social Research at the university and that offered me additional opportunities to work with colleagues in sociology and government on research topics involving race, economic justice, and the impact of government. This looked like an ideal setting to launch an academic career path! LaVera and I were also happy to be in the warmer climate of north Florida, where the cost of living was lower than it would have been in Massachusetts (where I also had job offers).

Our son, Adrian, was born in Tallahassee during our first year. So both family and my work at the university went well during the first couple of years. In my third year, I was delighted to learn that one of my professors at the University of Wisconsin had nominated me for a Brookings Economic Policy Fellowship. I submitted an application and was selected. Under the terms of the fellowship, I would work at a federal agency and participate in seminars at the Brookings Institution for fifteen months. Afterwards, I would return to my faculty position. The intent of the program was to foster a stronger relationship between academia and the federal government, and to improve federal economic policies. I went to work in the Research Department at the US Department of Housing and Urban Development.

One summer day nearing the end of my fellowship experience in Washington, DC, a colleague who I had met at one of the Brookings seminars approached me after our session.

"Mickey, I have watched you during our seminars and noticed how you have a way of making a point in a very diplomatic way," he said. "I think you would be very competitive for an administrative position that is open in the University of North Carolina (UNC) system." (Also known as the General Administration). I thanked him for the compliment, but thought, "This is not something that I want to do so early in my career; my plan is to work my way through the academic ranks—assistant professor, associate professor, and professor—over a period of years and then to consider a move into administration. The more I thought about and researched it, though, the more I began to understand that this opportunity was very special and unique. It would be a chance to work in the administration of President William C. Friday, one of the most revered and respected university presidents in America. When outstanding higher education leaders were being discussed, Friday's name was regularly mentioned in the same sentence with Father Theodore Hesburgh who led the University of Notre Dame for thirty-five years, and Clark Kerr, the first chancellor of the University of California, Berkeley and president of the University of California system. These three men were widely recognized as university leaders who took courageous stands and had a great impact on American higher education. The chance to work in Friday's administration would be a rare opportunity to observe excellent leadership from the inside and to learn from one of the best! Maybe I shouldn't dismiss it out of hand.

Still, it was not an easy decision. One of the objectives of top-level graduate programs like mine at UW Madison is to acculturate students into the profession. Not only are they taught the subject matter, research tools, and methodologies, but they're also taught the values of the academy. We were being prepared for a career of intellectual inquiry and subsequent publishing to add to the store of knowledge in the discipline—in my case, economics. The most successful students would publish in prestigious academic journals, and thereby gain professional acclaim for themselves and enhance the reputation of the graduate program that had trained them! Deviating from a traditional path to accomplish these things was to be done very reluctantly, if at all!

While still mulling this over a couple of weeks later, I received a call from my friend, Ed Fort. "Mickey," he said, "I've just been appointed chancellor of NC A&T State University and I want you to be part of my administration." He was referring to North Carolina Agricultural and Technical State University in Greensboro. "I'm still thinking about how to structure it and what particular role I would like for you to play, but it will likely be something in salary administration. We'll set the qualifications to be something like PhD in economics from a highly ranked university with a specialization in labor economics. Send me your curriculum vitae so that I can tailor the requirements for the job to match your background." Fort was a no-nonsense to-the-point kind of guy who could be very singularly focused.

"I'm honored, Ed. That sounds interesting; I'll get the CV in the mail to you," I replied.

He and I had met six or seven years earlier when I was a student in the PhD program at Wisconsin and he was chancellor of the University of Wisconsin Center System. Our families attended the same church. He was a Sunday School teacher and I served as Sunday School Superintendent. Hence, I had come to know him to be a family man of great faith and integrity, and who had a very high energy level.

Ed's overture about working in his administration came at a time when I was still struggling with disappointment and frustration over my department chair's decision to not recommend me for promotion and tenure without even discussing it with me. Once he explained it, I understood his logic, but was still miffed because he didn't talk with me about it beforehand. Also, the prospect of earning an administrative salary to better support my family had some appeal. In all honesty, however, I wasn't too excited about the possibility of landing a position in Ed's administration. Ed is a good man, and A&T is a great university, but again, I was unsure about abandoning my faculty path for an administrative path at this point in my career. Though I kept it to myself, my ambivalence drove me to be very deliberate and noncommittal in my response to Ed's initial call.

A few days after Ed's call, I went to Chapel Hill, North Carolina, to interview for a position in the University of North Carolina General Administration. I had decided that there was no harm in exploring options, since doing so would put me in a better position to choose the best career path forward. I thought that my day of interviews had gone well, but I just didn't know if I was ready to move into administration. At any rate, it was beginning to look like I might have two administrative job options in North Carolina.

Not long after my UNC General Administration interview, a member of the NC A&T search committee called. "Dr. Burnim," a friendly female voice said, "you have been selected as a finalist for the director of salary administration position at NC A&T and we would like for you to come to Greensboro for an on-campus interview." I was happy to receive this notification, but not surprised, because I knew that the job description had been tailored to my resumé.

"Thank you very much! That's exciting! I'd be delighted to come for an interview," I told her.

The interview went well, though I did detect a very slight raising of eyebrows by a couple of the committee members in reaction to one or two of my answers to their questions.

"Why do you think you're the best fit for this job?"

"Well, actually, I'm doing the interview to check you out just as you're checking me out. We'll both know more after the interview," I explained. I got the feeling that the search committee was looking for someone who was really excited about the prospect of working at NC A&T in addition to doing this job, and that they didn't quite find that excitement in me. They probably sensed my internal conflict about moving to administration and misinterpreted it as a lack of enthusiasm about NC A&T. In any case, I expected to be offered the job because Ed had told me that he wanted me in his administration.

After the two interviews, LaVera and I had a serious talk about what we wanted our future to look like. We tucked the kids into their respective beds and then retired to our own bedroom. We sat on the bed with our backs resting against the headboard as we often did when we wanted to have a really important discussion. "Babe, it looks like I might be offered both of these North Carolina jobs. How would you feel about moving yet once again?"

"I'm not sure," she said. "You know that I want to get an MBA and I was planning to apply to the Florida State University School of Business. Another move at this time would force me to postpone my plans."

Ultimately, we agreed that either Greensboro, NC, or the Research Triangle area would be a more desirable place to live and raise our young children, and would provide several excellent options for her to continue her education. "In the final analysis," she noted, "we can stay here or move to North Carolina. I can accomplish my goals either way. Where will you be happiest?"

I was learning that LaVera's selflessness was very nearly an unconscious reflection of her love—her very powerful love language!

I heard from the UNC General Administration job first. "Mickey, we'd like for you to join us here in the General Administration and an offer letter will be coming to you soon," Dr. Raymond Dawson, my prospective new boss, told me.

"Thank you! I really appreciate it; we will consider it very carefully once we receive it," I replied.

After the letter arrived with the terms of employment, benefits, and salary, LaVera and I discussed it somewhat excitedly. During that discussion, I realized that I had overcome my hesitancy about moving into administration and that I was probably going to accept one of the North Carolina jobs. Either North Carolina region would give us a more desirable environment for raising our two children—a much larger African American middle class for social interactions, and a career path that could lead to significant personal and professional growth, possibly even a college presidency.

Two weeks after my visit to NC A&T, I had still not heard anything from them. That was puzzling because they were only interviewing two or three finalists and I had been told to expect their decision within a week. Since the time for me to respond to the UNC offer was drawing near, I thought I would call Ed for a status report.

"Hello, Ed," I said, after his receptionist connected us. "How are you? It's been a couple of weeks since my visit and I thought I would call to see what's going on."

I detected a very slight pause on his end, maybe a hint of embarrassment, and then heard him say, "Mick, I've been meaning to call you. The committee did its work and submitted their recommendation to me. You were beaten out."

"What?" I said. "Someone was deemed more qualified for a job whose very description had been written based on my curriculum vitae?"

I felt torn between feeling disappointed at not being offered the job on the one hand, and being amused at the irony of someone being a better me than I was on the other hand! Life is indeed interesting!

Well, that did it. What began as a choice between two good alternatives turned out to be one job offer. One door had closed very unexpectedly but there was still one to consider. It just so happened that the offer in hand was the one I preferred. The General Administration position would give me a chance to work in the administration not only with William F. Friday, but with higher education leaders on all of the sixteen campuses of the University of North Carolina system. The sheer breadth and depth of this work experience had the potential to greatly expand my future career options over what they would be if I took a mid-level management job on a single campus. One of my personal rubrics for decision-making is to pursue decisions that expand my options rather than limit them, whenever possible. This likely would have led me to make the same decision had I actually had the two offers.

Hence, I accepted the UNC General Administration position and we moved to Durham, North Carolina. LaVera went on to earn her MBA at the University of North Carolina at Chapel Hill, both of our children had great formative primary and secondary school years, graduated from high school, and went on to college. The career path that I chose, going through the door that was open, led me to a thirty-five-year career in higher education administration, including leading four institutions as president or chancellor.

4

LEARNING ABOUT LEADERSHIP

It was during my time working in the UNC General Administration that I became a student of "leadership." My supervisor, Vice President Raymond H. Dawson, nominated me for participation in the Government Executives Institute, a leadership development program for North Carolina state government executives. For the program, a classroom full of managers from across state governments came together at the UNC Chapel Hill School of Business for two or three days per month for several months to study various facets of leadership. We were taught by faculty members from the School of Business and I was fascinated to discover a whole discipline of study called "leadership." For me, this was a wonderful introduction to principles of management, marketing, budgeting, strategic planning, and team-building.

We were introduced to such fascinating concepts and ideas as Maslow's hierarchy of needs, Richard Levin's financial management strategies, and the Myers-Briggs personality test. I was excited to discover Maslow's hierarchy as a powerful factor in individual motivation, the commanding simplicity of Richard Levin's "Buy Low, Sell High" financial wealth-building strategy, and insightful revelations about my Introverted, Observant, Thinking, and Judging (ISTJ) personality preferences using the Myers-Briggs indicator. I had always had a passion for learning new things, and I was exhilarated by the high probability that these tidbits and insights would help me become a highly effective leader!

My four-and-a-half years of service in the UNC General Administration marked a period of tremendous exposure and growth for me. Since I had no previous administrative experience, my learning curve for this new position was very steep. I knew nothing about budgeting, strategic planning, working with governing boards, hiring and personnel management, team building, establishing and nurturing relationships with state and federal legislators and administrators, or working with a myriad of interested parties including alumni, students, faculty, and donors. There were also the areas of marketing and working with the media, which a public leader needed to negotiate. My work in the UNC General Administration afforded me the chance to observe and assist the campuses in the UNC system in doing many of these things. Hence, I learned how to begin to practice these facets of leadership effectively and also how to avoid many of the mistakes that academic leaders on the campuses were making.

When I participated in the Government Executives Institute, I was one of the few, if not the only, participant whose current job did not involve supervising or managing other people. Because I had no people who reported to me, some members of the class teased me by saying, "You're just staff." I don't know whether this was intended as harmless fun at my expense or if it was a cruel attempt to make me feel that I didn't belong in the institute. In either case, as was my predisposition, I chose to take a positive perspective and receive it as good-natured banter. The Government Executives Institute experience was a very significant step in my intentional preparation for eventual leadership in higher education—perhaps even a presidency! One of the main reasons I had accepted the job in the UNC General Administration was that I saw it, potentially, as a great steppingstone along a very plausible path to a presidency, and I felt that the world the institute had opened for me would make that pathway even wider. I was greatly expanding my awareness of some of the knowledge and skills needed to be an effective leader, as well as some of my information and experience deficiencies. Consequently, I started building my personal library, choosing sessions at professional meetings, talking with higher education leaders with whom I came into contact, and observing leaders in the UNC system, all with the intent of filling in gaps in my knowledge of leadership principles and the requisite skills.

My parents had taught me during my formative years that I should always do my best at any task or endeavor that I undertook. The basis of the logic underpinning that dictum was really driven home to me by my UNC General Administration experience. I worked there four-and-a-half years with senior administrators and leaders on all of the sixteen campuses of the system, primarily with vice-chancellors for academic affairs, but also with some academic deans and department chairs and, occasionally, chancellors.

After almost four years, Dawson assigned me the lead responsibility for doing a system-wide evaluation of the business administration degree programs. This led to my having multiple meetings and contacts with business deans and faculty to move the agenda forward. One of my collaborators in this evaluation was the dean of the Business School at North Carolina Central University (NCCU), Dr. Tyronza Richmond, who, subsequent to the completion of the business programs review, emerged from the campus search process as the new chancellor of that university. I hadn't noticed anything special about my interactions with him until one day when he called me aside and said, "Mickey, I've been watching how you handle yourself in these meetings and I think you would make a good vice-chancellor for academic affairs. We're searching to fill that position and I would like for you to apply."

Wow! I thought. *This might actually lead somewhere!* A year earlier, I had been invited to apply for a vice presidency at Jackson State University in Mississippi, which I did. At the end of the process, I was offered the job. LaVera and I discussed it and she made herself very clear.

"It's a good opportunity and I don't want to stand in your way. But my children and I will not be moving to Mississippi!" She loved me and was supportive, but her love and support had limits! I appreciated her position and declined the offer.

With that history in mind, I was grateful to know that Richmond had been impressed with my work and thought that I might be the right person to serve as the chief academic officer in his administration! In telling LaVera about my conversation with Richmond that evening, I could barely contain my excitement. "Dear," I said, "the chief academic officer is generally recognized as the second in charge at any university—the first vice president or, in this case, vice-chancellor among equals! If I get this job, it would put me in the most likely direct line to a presidency than any other university position except the presidency itself!"

She responded, "That sounds great Babe. I'm proud of you! You should go for it!"

We had little inkling of the profound impact that such a job would have on our family life.

Though unexpected, this was a welcome overture, as it seemed right from several perspectives. First, the vice-chancellor for academic affairs position was a logical step from my then current position along a path to a presidency (chancellorship). In fact, a chief academic officer position like this one is the most traditional path to a university presidency. Second, this position would be in the UNC system and, therefore, would make my gains in leadership experience and knowledge maximally relevant. Third, the university was within a few miles of my home, and taking the position, if my candidacy were successful, would cause no disruption to the established routines and activities of my family. It appeared to be a fantastic opportunity and a coveted steppingstone!

While trying to keep a lid on my excitement, I quickly submitted my application for the job. As the search process played out, I was invited for a campus visit with the search committee as one of the finalists. I don't remember whether it was during this campus visit or at some other point during the process, but the search committee chair pointedly told me, "Mickey, you are not the most qualified applicant, but you're the one the chancellor wants."

His declaration gave me two strong messages. First, the chancellor had communicated to him that I was his first choice. Second, the chair let me know that he didn't agree with the chancellor's choice. I chose to allow the first message to buoy my spirit. I thought, *This might actually happen!* His revelation was thrilling, but I had learned not to assume that what seemed to be happening would actually come to fruition, so I tempered my excitement and filed away the second message. If I actually did get this job, the committee chair would be my campus colleague.

Surely enough, the job of vice-chancellor for academic affairs at NCCU was offered to me. I accepted it and began work August 1, 1986. The performance of my duties and responsibilities, as well as dealing with the myriad challenges the job presented, provided the first large incubator for the development of my leadership philosophy and approaches. This experience also contributed heavily to the shaping and sharpening of the lenses through which I would perceive and practice effective leadership. I served in this role for nine years, under three different chancellors, and annually directly supervised an average of eleven professional staff, including academic deans for seven schools and colleges, the university registrar, the director of admissions, and two associate vice-chancellors. This is the job that first brought me face-to-face with the vagaries of hiring and firing, planning and evaluating, supervising, coaching and counseling, encouraging and advising, team-building and motivating.

My experience to this point had taught me two very important lessons:

1) Even though leaders don't have to be experts in everything, they need to have at least broad knowledge about the critical aspects of their organizations' inner workings.
2) You cannot put too much emphasis on always doing your best. You never know who is watching or how their perceptions will affect your future opportunities!

Learning About Leadership at NCCU

"Mickey, this university is like a big ship that's cruising along. We're going to do our best to change its course for about five years. Then we'll turn it over to someone else."

This is what Richmond said to me as I sat in front of his desk one morning during my first week on the job as a member of his executive leadership team. His office was on the first floor of the Hoey Administration Building, which was at least forty years old. Nothing much marked it as the chancellor's office except for a private restroom concealed by the left-side door behind his desk, and two large windows to his right. These looked out toward the statue of the university's founder, Dr. James E. Shepard, which stood in the traffic circle in front of the building.

Chancellor Richmond was an average-sized man of medium height who sported a cropped full beard that refused to stay within the imaginary lines on his face that would have merited the label "neat." It was salt-and-pepper gray, and blended in with the hair on top of his head. His usual demeanor was one of pleasant calmness conveyed with a placid smile. He prided himself on not letting things rankle him.

I had just begun my job as vice-chancellor and he was sharing his vision for the difference he wanted to make during his turn at leading the university. "We want to empower the faculty . . . give them a greater voice in the affairs of the university and focus more on the well-being of our students," he told me. The university's student enrollment was flat to declining, and the state appropriations were inadequate for compensating faculty appropriately or tending to the maintenance of existing facilities and the construction of necessary new ones. "This won't be easy," he told me, "But we'll give it five years and see what happens."

I came away from that meeting thinking about the enormity of the challenge that we faced but, more importantly, with a deep commitment to do my part. I would lead the division of academic affairs so that the channels of communication were broadly open to faculty and we could receive their input and keep them informed. We could do this thing!

The first two or three years proved just how prescient Richmond's ship analogy was. The enrollment challenge persisted even though we focused a lot of attention on student recruitment and retention. We hired external enrollment management consultants, developed an enrollment management plan, and worked the plan. The university's state budget didn't improve very much either. I and other members of Richmond's leadership team made numerous trips to Raleigh, the state capitol, to describe our needs to legislators in their offices or the hallways of their office buildings. We felt like our message was getting through, but the results were slow in coming.

I found the first few months in this new job to be exhilarating! *Wow*, I thought. *This is really fun!* I got into the office between 8 and 8:30 each morning and usually left to go home between 6 and 7 pm. The job had no regular hours though. The leadership team accepted the reality that we had to give whatever the job demanded. Sometimes, like board meeting days or commencements, we needed to arrive by 7 am. At times, when a critical report was due to the regional accreditor, or the system president's office, we stayed on campus working into the wee hours of the morning. The pace was brutal and unrelenting. There was always something else to get done and too little time for reflection and slowing down. A faculty member spoke to me at a reception one day and asked, "How's it going?"

Revealing just a hint of the pride I felt, I replied, "I'm putting in ten-to-twelve hour days, working really hard and it doesn't seem like I'll ever catch up." He looked me in the eye and pointedly said, "You can work yourself into a heart attack and die, and they'll have someone else in your chair within two weeks, and people will barely remember that you were here!"

That really got my attention, and I knew that he was right. I needed to learn how to set a more sustainable pace, focusing more on what was important—those things that were critical for the development and growth of the university, and less on what was urgent—demands from others that would satisfy an immediate need they had. I then recalled how several former colleagues in the UNC system administration had shared their regret at not spending more time with their children during their formative years and how determined I had been not to make the same mistake. Hence, I made special efforts to attend Cinnamon's and Adrian's school programs and athletic contests. I even coached Cinnamon's softball team and Adrian's baseball team. I continued to do my best to meet the critical demands of the job while remaining aware of, and prioritizing, my family responsibilities. The struggle to maintain the desired work-life balance never went away.

Two of our special challenges were the university's law school and nursing program. The law school was founded during a period of legal segregation to provide opportunities for African American students to become lawyers. As our society changed and desegregation became a goal for higher education, more Black students enrolled in traditionally White universities, but White students were also attracted to opportunities at the HBCUs. This led to a problem for the NCCU School of Law, because the growing number of applications from White students made it harder for African American students to secure a spot in the entering cohorts. The law school could fill its classes each year, but it was harder and harder for Black students, who came disproportionately from disadvantaged educational and socioeconomic backgrounds, to win slots. How to serve the traditional mission of the law school in a desegregated environment? This was one huge challenge that Richmond and I worked with the law school dean to address. There was no magic solution to the challenge, but a number of strategies helped to improve it. We worked harder to raise scholarship money so that disadvantaged students could devote more of their time to studying rather than having to work to pay tuition, fees, and living expenses. The dean and law faculty created a performance-based program that allowed conditionally admitted students whose backgrounds suggested possible struggle during the first year to be introduced to legal writing and the rigors of law school to demonstrate their potential for success. This program yielded some positive results.

A related but different challenge was the nursing program. Many students enrolled in the university with the dream of becoming a nurse, a requirement of which was to earn the bachelor of science in nursing degree and pass the nursing licensure examination. Most students were able to pass their courses and progress through the program to the point of earning their degrees. On the other hand, significant numbers of our nursing students found it difficult to pass the national licensure examination the first time they took it. For the state board of nursing to approve a nursing program, a high percentage of students had to pass the national licensure examination on their first try. The passing standard was changed frequently, but its stated purpose was to "reflect the amount of nursing ability currently required to practice competently at the entry level." For a host of reasons, African American students tended to pass in lower percentages on their first attempt. Hence, the approval of the nursing program seemed to constantly be under scrutiny and "warning" or "probation." This challenge was not unique to NCCU, but was present at practically all of the nursing schools at HBCUs. It would lead to a defining issue for Richmond's tenure at NCCU.

One morning Richmond asked his office assistant to call me to his office. As I walked down the two flights of stairs to the first floor, I wondered exactly what was up. "Good morning," I greeted him as I walked into his office.

"Good morning," he responded from behind his desk with his usual smile, but I noticed it immediately turned into a quizzical, distressed look as he turned to gaze out of his window. "Mickey, I just received a call from the system president. He told me that he has decided to close our nursing program and merge it with Fayetteville State's. A press release announcing it will go out within the hour."

"What?" My response was barely audible.

"He didn't even give me the courtesy of telling me that he was considering this action or asking what I thought," Richmond seemed hurt and incensed by what he saw as a disrespectful affront to him as the institution's leader, and as a man, even more so than the actual loss of the nursing program. This kind of abrupt unilateral action was the exact opposite of the slow, deliberative, and consultative approach that was customary and so highly valued in academe. It was, however, well in line with the way things were done in the business world.

This system president had succeeded the legendary Bill Friday. The board of governors had deliberately sought a nontraditional president, one who would bring a more "business-like" approach to leading the university system. The new president, Clemmie Dixon (C. D.) Spangler, filled that bill. He was reputed to be a billionaire businessman who had grown up in North Carolina and would run the university "like a business." He had an MBA from the Harvard Business School, sat on a number of corporate boards, and had even chaired one of Harvard's major fundraising campaigns. He was a powerful White man who knew how big business worked and could apply that model to a university system. He also knew how to make decisions. "I'll make decisions fairly quickly and if we subsequently need to change course. Hopefully, we'll have time to do that," he shared with the general administration staff on his first day as UNC president.

Undoubtedly, he saw the nursing programs at NCCU and Fayetteville State as problems that needed fixing. Both were struggling with National Council Licensure Examination passing rates, but North Carolina needed more nurses. It's not clear with whom he consulted or over what period of time, but the president made what seemed to us to be one of his quick decisions.

"Ty, I understand your being miffed at the way the president has done this. He really should have told you what he was considering and given you a chance to express your view before his final decision," I told him. "Managing the nursing program takes a lot of energy and resources that we could easily put into other programs and needs. I know you have to protest his decision, but I suggest that you not protest too much." I continued making a play on Queen Gertrude's line in Shakespeare's *Hamlet*. I selfishly saw it as an opportunity to let a major headache go away and have the blame fall to someone else. Richmond smiled at my suggestion, but didn't comment.

In retrospect, I can see that Richmond was much more deeply offended by the president's handling of this episode than I initially realized. He went quietly about contacting members of the North Carolina General Assembly, particularly members of its Black Caucus, and asking for their support of the NCCU nursing program and their help in getting Spangler's decision reversed. His choice to enlist the help of legislators was extremely potent since NCCU had a number of alumni who were serving in the general assembly. Their political power was consequential due to their numbers, seniority, and leadership positions. Two examples are Delegate H. M. "Mickey" Michaux who had served as the first Black US attorney in the South since Reconstruction and had twelve years in the general assembly, and Delegate Dan Blue who was the first Black speaker of the House of Delegates since Reconstruction. Though I was not a witness to any of those discussions, I had the distinct impression that those representatives and their colleagues made it very clear to the president, his staff, and members of the UNC Board of Governors, that they wanted the decision to merge the NCCU nursing program reversed, and that failure to do so could jeopardize the UNC state appropriation. The decision was reversed and NCCU still has its nursing program to this day.

Richmond's campaign to save the nursing program was successful, but it came at tremendous cost. He knew that actively opposing the president's decision made his continued service as chancellor untenable because he had publicly opposed his boss and won. Not long after the decision had been reversed, Richmond summoned me to his office. After I was seated in one of the chairs facing his desk, with a pensive look on his face, he told me, "Mickey, I'm going to resign and go back to my faculty slot in the school of business." A shock wave went through my body. I felt a sense of imminent loss. Richmond had been a good leader for NCCU. He was quiet and gentle with his ever-present smile. He had proven to be a man of great integrity, always seeking to do what was right. He had also demonstrated that he was a man of courage and strength. At my core, I understood the internal dynamics that led him to this decision, but I had to protest anyway. "Ty, don't be hasty. You're doing an outstanding job of leading this university, and you have a lot of support among faculty, staff, and alumni," I said.

He nodded slightly in agreement but added, "My plan from the beginning was to try it for five years. It has been a little more than five and the time is right."

Richmond's resignation was effective in December, just a few months after the nursing decision reversal. Upon learning of his resignation, the system president was heard to say, "He's a wise man."

Ty Richmond announced his resignation at a press conference soon thereafter, and people immediately started asking me if I would be the heir apparent to the NCCU chancellorship. I was in the second-most powerful and influential position at the university and had earned the respect of some of the key faculty and staff. I felt that I was ready to take on this mantle of leadership, but that it was too early to voice this or encourage speculation about my possible candidacy. Hence, when approached, I deflected with something like, "There hasn't been time to get over the shock of Chancellor Richmond's decision. We should let that sink in and see where things lead."

For two or three weeks following Richmond's press conference, the president's office was silent regarding the process for finding a replacement. Finally, his public relations staff announced that the Board of Trustees would initiate a formal search process in the spring and that an interim chancellor would be named to serve from the date of Richmond's departure until a new chancellor was named. I and a number of other people were surprised when the interim chancellor was announced. She enjoyed a reputation as a bright young scholar and had served as assistant vice president for academic affairs in the office of the president for a couple of years or so. She was short in stature and had a very bubbly personality. She was also a very quick study, and grasped important nuances and implications immediately. She held a PhD from a major university and had served as a faculty member at one of the UNC constituent universities. As I recall, that was the sum total of her administrative experience and that, along with her youth, was why I saw her as an unexpected choice to lead NCCU for the year or so that the search was expected to take. Initially, I felt personally rejected, indeed affronted, that a person who appeared to be much less well-prepared for the job was chosen over me. I assuaged my disappointment by telling myself that the president might have made this choice so that my possible consideration for the permanent chancellorship would remain open. Often, the interim person is prohibited from consideration for the permanent job.

I had learned that circumstances and situations can change very quickly, making it difficult for a leader to maintain his or her equilibrium. A good leader definitely needs to be able to deal with change appropriately.

THE SEARCH FOR A NEW LEADER

After the interim chancellor had begun her service, the president authorized the NCCU Board of Trustees to begin the process to find a permanent replacement for Richmond. The call for applications and nominations went out to academic institutions across the country and a colleague from one of them called me and asked, "Mickey, I think you would be great for this. Would you like for me to nominate you?"

"I really appreciate your saying that. Yes, I would be honored for you to nominate me."

The vetting of applicants and nominees went along normally and, after a few months, the names of finalists were released as they were being invited for interviews. I was surprised and disappointed to see that my name was not among them. How could the search committee not have included me? I had served in the provost position for five years and was generally recognized as having done a solid job. No one on the list of finalists had more relevant experience in higher education, and none of them knew as much about the university, its culture, or its challenges as I did. *What was going on here?* I wondered.

The NCCU Faculty Senate leadership was also perplexed. Its chair, Dr. Bernice Johnson, publicly questioned how finalists for the chancellorship could be selected for interviews and the university's own provost not be invited for an interview. It didn't take long for me to figure out what had happened. I surmised that well-meaning power brokers—the president, Speaker Dan Blue, Representative Mickey Michaux, and others—who wanted the best for NCCU had decided that one person in particular was just the right person to lead the university at that time, and they were determined to hire that person. I believe they wanted to overshadow the negative pall that hung over the university, largely because of the public administration program fiasco which had been a major embarrassment for the university and the nursing program struggles, by bringing in a leader with a national reputation for excellence, some of which would automatically be conferred to the university with the appointment. They wanted a luminary whose mere presence would project strength, integrity, and respect on the institution. That person was Julius L. Chambers, Esq. At that time, he was executive director of the NAACP Legal Defense and Education Fund Inc., but had earned his reputation by being the first African American to attend, and graduate first in his class from, the University of North Carolina Law School. He went on to wage a distinguished and effective legal fight against segregation in the United States. Chambers was small in stature, about five feet six inches or so, but was a giant in civil rights litigation and, therefore, known throughout the country!

After the search had been completed, the president, standing at the podium in a board of governors' meeting to introduce Chambers as the new chancellor, told the board members, visitors, and others who had assembled for the announcement: "We flew up to New York and met with Attorney Chambers to explain to him what a difference he would make to NCCU and to convince him to answer the call to lead his alma mater, and we're glad that he did."

Chambers allowed his name to be entered into the search process and accepted the job even though he loved practicing law, did not intend to stop, and declared that he would only lead the university for a period of time. "I don't intend to retire as chancellor," he declared. And he didn't.

Chambers' becoming chancellor of NCCU seemed to have the hoped-for effect, particularly among people outside the university. The board of governors that had appointed him, the North Carolina General Assembly, especially the Black Caucus, and the North Carolina corporate community overall strongly supported his arrival. The general assembly accepted the upgraded request and funded what is now home to the Julius L. Chambers Biomedical and Biotechnology Research Institute. Whereas the board of governors had previously stuck pretty rigidly to its queue system for requesting funding from the general assembly for capital projects among the constituent institutions, it quickly supported Chambers' request to change a building renovation project to a completely new building!

    He was also successful at increasing private fundraising for the university. At one point, it seemed that North Carolina's leading corporations were lining up to make gifts. I recall one occasion when Chambers and I stood next to each other at a reception where a bank was about to present him a check for several hundred thousand dollars for scholarships. With his arms folded across his chest, Chambers covered his mouth and chin with his left hand while holding his left elbow in his right hand. He often struck this pose when deep in thought while standing. Showing a great deal of satisfaction with the smile partially hidden by his hand, he whispered to me, "I sued all of these guys." He referred to a series of civil rights and employment law suits that he had filed over decades. All of the external indicators were favorable and, from that perspective, those leaders who had recruited him had been right. His leadership lifted the visibility and the profile of his alma mater.

    This episode illustrates that sometimes influential people who care about an organization will, seeking the best outcome, use their influence to affect the selection of a leader. In such cases, what is happening behind the scenes is more consequential that what is happening center stage!

Working with the New Chancellor

Just as the peaceful appearance of a duck swimming on the surface of a pond contrasts greatly with the frenetic paddling of its feet below the surface, those of us inside NCCU became painfully aware of the more challenging aspects of Chancellor Chambers' leadership. Toward the end of his first week as chancellor, I ran into one of my vice-chancellor colleagues in the stairwell of the administration building. Except for us, the stairwell was vacant. Cocking his head slightly to one side as a somber expression came across his face, he said, "Mickey, I don't know. This new chancellor is something else! He told me that he's letting me go, and I understand that he has said the same thing to two of our other colleagues." All four of us had been colleagues on Richmond's team since early in his administration. I shook my head slowly from side to side in commiseration.

"What did he tell you?" he asked me.

"He told me, 'Mickey, I'm going to keep you . . . for now, but I'll be reassessing that as we go along.'"

During his first week on the job, he fired three members of the chancellor's cabinet and put a fourth one, me, on notice that I would be monitored continuously to determine my employment disposition. I felt insulted by his threat, yet thankful that I had not been dealt the same fate as my colleagues. Clearly, he had come to campus with his mind made up about key personnel changes that he would make. I never knew why I was given a chance to prove myself and my colleagues were not. The unfairness of this approach made a lasting impression on me and shaped my thinking about leadership transitions. Unless there was a strong need for an immediate change, I would give people a chance to prove their compatibility with my vision, values, and goals!

Serving as vice-chancellor for academic affairs in Chambers' administration stretched and challenged me like an earthworm being pulled from a mother bird's beak by her hatchlings in the nest. Not having been socialized into the world of academic administration, Chambers could not understand and did not accept the slow deliberate pace at which things moved. He had already announced that he did not intend to stay in the chancellorship until retirement, so he felt real urgency to get things done quickly.

When he asked me how long it would take to revise the general education curriculum and I told him two years, he wanted to know why it would be so long. Since my commitment to him was the same as it had been to Richmond and the interim Chancellor before—to contribute all I could to the success of his leadership—I asked myself, *How might we expedite the curriculum revision process and remain true to the academic values of collegiality and shared governance, while not doing harm to the continuing work of teaching and research by our faculty?*

I mulled this over and came up with a different approach that I thought might work. With the chancellor's approval, I offered key faculty members stipends to meet with me on Saturday mornings to develop the new curriculum. The Saturday meetings would minimize conflicts with regularly scheduled classes and provide added incentive for faculty participation. That faculty members comprised the majority of the curriculum committee assured compliance with the collegiality and shared governance values of academe. I thought this was an elegant solution to the chancellor's challenge, if it would only work!

The committee worked consecutive Saturday mornings for a few weeks and hammered out a new curriculum that focused on competencies and content rather than courses, incorporating cutting-edge thought about curriculum design. And since faculty had been so intimately involved throughout, the new curriculum was successfully moved through the campus approval process! Though it had its detractors, the university used the new curriculum for more than ten years. I remain very proud of that successful creative approach.

One day Chambers summoned me to his office on the first floor of the administration building. His assistant ushered me into his office and directed me to one of the armchairs facing his desk. He sat in his leather executive chair behind the desk reading his mail and signing letters. Without taking his attention away from the stack of papers that he was working on, he spoke: "Mickey, do you know anything about using transfer students to build enrollment?"

"Yes, I do."

He then lifted his eyes from the papers in front of him and looked directly at me. "How many transfer students do we get annually?"

"Transfers make up about 5 percent of our enrollment each year—somewhere between 400 and 600 students," I stated confidently as I leaned forward in my chair and returned his gaze.

"How many of them are from North Carolina?" He refocused his eyes on his paperwork.

"About 90 percent, somewhere between 350 and 500."

"How many are from Virginia?"

"I'm not sure."

"How many are from South Carolina?"

"I don't have those numbers off the top of my head and will have to get back to you."

He then looked up from his paperwork again, gave a slight smile, and said, "Oh, I see. You'll have to get back to me." I felt like I had just been in a contest of wits with Chambers challenging my competency and interpreting my admission that I didn't have all the data he asked about on the tip of my tongue as my waving a white flag!

This became a pattern for many of our one-on-one interactions and I would leave them exhausted and feeling I had been cross-examined! Given the early meeting when he put me on notice, these sessions felt like he was trying to prove to himself and demonstrate to me that I should be let go also!

I should have been forewarned earlier when a former high-level executive at the NAACP Legal Defense and Education Fund said to me, "You are in for an interesting time because Julius is an extreme micromanager!"

This incidental meeting happened at a wedding after Chambers had been announced as the next chancellor, but before he took office. We were seated at the reception along with the other guests and the atmosphere was as would be expected after a wedding ceremony. The room was buzzing with lively conversations, so to make sure I didn't miss anything, I slid into the seat next to the official and asked her directly, "What do you mean when you say he is an extreme micromanager?"

She chuckled, half to herself. "You'll see." And that was the end of the conversation.

After Chambers had been on the job a few months, I made another one of my visits to his office. While working on his stack of mail, he asked me, "How do other universities deal with students who don't quite meet the admissions standards but have potential? Students from poor families who haven't been well served by the public schools?"

"Are you asking what kind of provisional admissions policies universities similar to ours have?"

"Yes, I guess so."

"Well, I'll poll some of our sister institutions in the UNC system and give you a report."

"Ok. Good."

Less than a week later, we were sitting in one of Chambers' cabinet meetings, which were now held in the faculty and staff dining room. Under Richmond and Benson, cabinet meetings had been held in the executive conference room on the third floor of the administration building. The executive conference room had a large conference table that could comfortably accommodate ten to twelve people, and it was conveniently located in the same building as almost all of the chancellor's direct reports. Chambers had expanded the list of invitees to his cabinet meetings from the six or seven people who reported to him directly to around twenty people, including several persons who reported to the vice chancellors. Hence, more space was needed for cabinet meetings. The faculty and staff dining room was a stand-alone building about a three-minute walk from the administration building. It served as both a lunch venue and a lounge for faculty and staff. The room was outfitted with a food buffet near the front, a few square tables for four on one side, and a couple of sitting areas including sofas, upholstered armchairs, and coffee tables on the other side, and one or two hassocks that people propped their feet on. During these meetings, Chambers would elicit reports and give assignments to whomever he chose. I, for one, was not at all happy with this arrangement. It had the effect of flattening out the chain of command, or channels of communication, perhaps yielding greater efficiency from the chancellor's perspective, but serving to undermine my authority and foster confusion. How could I hold one of my direct reports accountable if she had to spend time carrying out directives from the chancellor? How would I manage the work in my division of the university if my people were taken from their regular duties and responsibilities to carry out special orders from the chancellor? But, of course, he was the chancellor and could do whatever he pleased.

On this particular day, there were more than twenty people crowded into the dining room. People sat wherever they could—some in upholstered chairs, some in folding chairs, and some even on hassocks, as I recall. There was no order in the seating arrangements, as everyone just tried to position themselves so they could see the chancellor. Chambers presided over the meeting and went around the room seemingly at random asking people questions and giving out assignments. He had brought his stack of office mail to the meeting and opened it, read it, and assigned people to respond right there in the cabinet meeting! At one point, he suddenly looked up as if he was just reminded of something. "Nancy, I want you to research how other universities handle provisional admits and provide me a report." He was making the same assignment that he had given me just a few days ago to one of my direct reports!

The frustration that had been building inside me for months suddenly exploded in a spontaneous outburst: "What are you doing? That's the same assignment you gave me a few days ago and I'm already working on it! We don't both need to be working on the same assignment!" The room became quiet as people processed what had just happened. I had just confronted the chancellor with uncontrolled frustration in the presence of a room full of people. Had I just, unwittingly, tendered my resignation?

After the meeting, Chancellor Chambers summoned me to his office.

Oh my, I thought. *This is it! He's going to fire me now.* When I entered this time, he was looking directly at me and, with apparent sincerity, asked, "What's the problem?"

"You gave me that assignment a few days ago and before I have a chance to finish it, you give it to someone else who reports to me. It creates chaos and makes it harder for me to lead my division."

I don't remember the rest of the conversation, but note that he didn't fire me. I now understood very clearly just what the Legal Defense and Education Fund official meant when she told me he was a micromanager, and I also had great appreciation for the adverse impact that this kind of behavior could have on a leadership team!

The handling of leadership transitions and the negative effects of micromanagement were two important lessons that I learned when working with Chambers. I also saw firsthand how to effectively leverage one's passion for making a positive difference. Chambers had grown up in a family of limited economic means. He told the story of how his father, an automobile mechanic, was cheated by a customer who wouldn't pay for work done because his father couldn't get competent legal representation. Hence, Chambers decided to become a lawyer so he could represent poor people and people of color. In addition, he was known for being bold in his advocacy, as seen in his decision to ask for a building rather than just a renovation for his *alma mater*. His life was a lesson in relentless advocacy for those less fortunate and striving for excellence in all undertakings.

Early one Monday morning, Chambers appeared at the open door to my office and commanded: "Mickey, come down to my office; I need to discuss something with you." He had walked right past my secretary's desk without giving her a chance to announce his arrival.

This visit was completely unexpected. He had seldom come to my office in the two and a half years that he had been chancellor. I'm sure I could have counted those visits on one hand. Had I unknowingly said or done something to raise his ire? I didn't think so but couldn't be certain.

"Sure, I'll be right there," I said.

As I walked into his office, he was already seated at his desk and started to talk as soon as I walked in. "The president is going to call you in a few minutes and ask you to go to Elizabeth City State to serve as interim chancellor, and I think you should take it."

I felt as if I had been doused with a bucket of ice water. Every fiber of my being suddenly felt at full alert, experiencing shock, excitement, fear, and joy all at once! The prospect of serving as interim chancellor came about suddenly and unexpectedly, offering the possibility of being my own boss in leading a university! This sounded like the answer to my prayers for a better work situation. I felt well-prepared but suspected that it would be a challenging situation. I thanked Chambers for the information and went back to my office, mulling over these thoughts and emotions.

In short order, the office telephone rang, my secretary answered it, and buzzed me on the intercom: "The president is on the line for you."

"Hello. How are you this morning?" I tried to say cheerfully.

"I'm fine, Mickey and hope that you are. I need you to come over to my office so we can discuss an important matter. Did the chancellor tell you to expect my call?"

"Yes, he did. I'll be there in about twenty minutes."

After his administrative assistant had ushered me into his office, the president gestured for me to take one of the seats facing his desk and wasted no time in getting right to the point. "The chancellor at Elizabeth City State is leaving at the end of the month and I want you to go and serve as interim chancellor while the board of trustees searches for a permanent chancellor."

"Mr. President, I'm honored to be asked, but I'll need to pray about it and discuss it with my wife."

"That's fine but you'll need to do it quickly. The chancellor's last day is Thursday, and I need you to take over on Friday morning. Also, if you accept this assignment, I plan to send a friend and colleague that has worked for me before to serve as your assistant. You and he could take a "good cop/ bad cop" approach to leading the institution."

"Why would you do that? I don't need someone assigned to help me make difficult decisions or carry them out!"

"Well, you're a nice guy and some hard personnel decisions might be necessary. It might be better for someone other than you to take the blame. Anyway, that's what I plan to do."

This last declaration troubled me. I didn't want someone forced on me in this manner, even if it was allegedly to make things easier for me. Under some circumstances, this would have been a deal breaker; but I had been hoping and praying for relief from my current work situation and that prospect far outweighed the imposition of an assistant I didn't know and did not want.

After a full day of work at NCCU on Thursday, I drove the two hundred miles to Elizabeth City, spent the night in a local inn, and drove to the administration building on the Elizabeth City State University campus by eight o'clock the next morning.

Building the Leadership Team

Walking into the chancellor's office at Elizabeth City State University (ECSU) on Friday morning September 1, 1995, I felt really excited . . . almost giddy. On Monday, the UNC system president had summoned me to his office in Chapel Hill and officially asked me to serve as interim chancellor. Even though it was just a temporary assignment, a very strong sense of relief and gratitude came over me, so much so that I felt like doing cartwheels from the office door across the room to the chancellor's desk.

God had finally answered my prayer! I had been liberated from two and a half years of laboring in a kind of "work hell" where, instead of collegial conversations, I had been cross-examined and criticized for following established and time-honored values and procedures of the academy. I had been subjected to humiliation from my boss, the chancellor, who gave assignments to and received reports from my supervisees in his "expanded" cabinet meetings. Now I was on a campus where I was in charge! I would no longer have an on-campus supervisor and would be free to make final decisions about direction for the university, its pace of change, and the kind of work climate we would have! *Thank you, Jesus!*

My new office was located in the university's administration building. It was a modern structure that had been constructed in a "V" shape as a visual tribute to its athletic teams, the Vikings. The building entrance was at the point of the V and I was greeted as I opened the door of the building that morning.

"Good morning. Welcome to Elizabeth City State University!" said Jean Sims, the executive assistant to the chancellor, whom I had met on previous visits to the university. She escorted me to the chancellor's suite on the third floor and introduced me to the rest of the office staff. The chancellor's office itself sat at the top of the left side of the V. The entry door to the office faced outward toward the end of the left side, and the chancellor's desk was positioned at the end of the leg and facing the door. The office was spacious and deep, spanning about fifty feet from the door to the end of the V leg. It was awash in sunlight that shone through the windows lining both sides of the office. In spite of my exhilaration, I resisted the temptation to cartwheel my way to the desk because I didn't want to make an initial bad impression on my new office staff—that and the fact that I didn't know how to do cartwheels!

I sat in the pastel-pink leather executive chair behind the desk and took in the room from this vantage point. Two brown leather armchairs were positioned directly in front of the desk. To the right, along the back wall, was a sitting area for receiving visitors in a comfortable and informal manner. There was a couch along the wall, a coffee table, and a couple of upholstered armchairs. Between my desk and this sitting area, along the row of large windows, was an impressive rectangular wooden conference table surrounded by six brown leather armchairs. *This is really nice*, I thought. That was when I noticed the three-inch stack of papers on my desk just to the left of the ink blotter.

"What's this?" I asked my executive assistant.

"Those are requisitions for IT equipment and supplies. Mr. Taylor, the IT office director, brought them over yesterday and asked that I call them to your attention this morning. He says they're urgent!"

As I thumbed through the stack of requisitions, it quickly became obvious that these requests totaled more than $200,000! This would be a very large expenditure from this small university's budget and we simply could not afford to make a mistake. At that point, I decided to call the director of administrative computing into my office to have him explain these requests and how he would prioritize them.

"Please explain these requisitions," I asked when he arrived. "That's a lot of money for us to spend at one time. Can you rank order them?"

The director, a tall man who appeared to be in his early sixties, sat up straight in his chair and, with a hint of smugness, said, "Let me tell you. Yes, IT shops are expensive. Hardware and software are expensive, and organizations, including this university, are growing more and more dependent on them. Leading thinkers these days are saying that an organization needs to dedicate a fixed portion of its budget to IT, up to five percent, and spend that every year. And that's what you need to do. I'm the expert here and this is what I think we need to purchase for our university."

I thanked him for his insight and told him that I would get back to him.

It was clear that I needed someone with IT expertise to review these requisitions and advise me as to whether or not I should approve them . . . someone that I knew and trusted. John N. Smith came to mind immediately. Our families had worshiped together at St. Joseph's African Methodist Episcopal Church, where we were members during the thirteen years we lived in Durham. And, for a period, John served on the board of trustees for NCCU when I was provost. He and I also worked on the church's finance committee together. John had spent a quick twenty-five years working as a high-powered manager for IBM and he had his retirement Rolex to prove it. Not only did he know about IT hardware, software, and systems, but he had management experience at one of the world's foremost IT companies!

I called John that afternoon. "John, I began my service as interim chancellor at Elizabeth City State today and I need your help."

As was his style, John's response was short and to the point, "What do you need?"

"I have a stack of requisitions for IT equipment and software that totals hundreds of thousands of dollars and I need you to assess it and advise me as to what I should do. You could do it in a couple of days."

"Sure, I'll do that for you," he kindly consented. John's affirmative response gave me a sense of both accomplishment and comfort. He had the necessary background to do the assessment and advise me, and I knew him to be a man of integrity because of my church work with him. I could trust his advice.

John reviewed the requisitions and then met with the administrative computing director to discuss them. As I expected, John was not intimidated by the director's aggressiveness in advocating for his requests and ended up advising me to approve a portion of the total, which I did. This process reinforced the wisdom of seeking advice from a trusted third party and led me to conclude that John would be a wonderful addition to my leadership team if I could attract him.

"John, your counsel and advice were just what I needed and I really appreciate the way you met with the director in ascertaining the facts to formulate your advice. I could really benefit from your help on a continuing basis. Would you consider joining me in leading this university during this interim period?" I asked.

One reason I had thought to consult with him in the first place was that he had shared with me at church that he was severing ties with the company that he had begun working for after he retired from IBM. He told me that the president of that company, to whom he reported, lacked integrity and he could no longer work for her. John was still a young man, in his mid to late fifties, had a wealth of management, leadership, and IT experience, and was a person of faith whom I could trust. The salary I could offer him was about fifty percent of what the job market would require, but John agreed to take the job for what we could pay.

John was my first hire at ECSU. His job title of "assistant to the president" was intended to give him broad latitude to work on a variety of problems and issues and to advise me on anything that might arise. Not long after John came aboard, the administrative computing director decided to leave the university, so I asked John to manage the university's IT operations for me. He led us in developing a comprehensive plan for our IT operations and helped foster a closer and more cooperative working relationship between our academic and administrative computing shops. As a member of my cabinet, John attended all its meetings and sat near the head of the table at my right hand. This symbolic positioning and his proclivity to honor my desire for all cabinet members to participate fully in the discussion, as well as the soundness and reasonableness of his observations and suggestions, propelled him into the role of a de facto chief-of-staff. The vice-chancellors and other direct reports on the cabinet began to recognize him as one whose opinion I valued highly and started to run ideas by him prior to introducing them at the cabinet meetings. My first appointment in building my own leadership team had served to strengthen the team through helping to communicate a clearer vision of our leadership, values, work ethic, and expectations.

One day, I was meeting with a distinguished alumna of the university, Dr. Jeanette Hawkins Evans, who was also a leading donor. She had grown up in Eastern North Carolina and, after graduating from ECSU, went on to serve for about forty years in the Baltimore City public school system. Many of those years, she taught English, but retired as a highly valued administrator whose last job was chief of staff for the superintendent. As I found to be true with many of the university's alumni, Evans was fiercely loyal to her alma mater. She was active in the national alumni association, leading many of their fundraising efforts over the years. She returned to campus often for homecomings, convocations, and athletic events, cheered for the athletic teams when they competed in her area, and was usually among the first and most generous in contributing to the university's scholarship funds.

"Dr. Burnim, you know that I love this university and want to see it grow and prosper," she said at our meeting. "I think that you've made a good start in your leadership and I appreciate it. I'm planning to retire from the Baltimore City Public Schools soon. Feel free to call on me whenever you think I can be of service to my alma mater."

"Why thank you, Dr. Evans! I will certainly do that!" This started the wheels turning in my head. *Maybe I could convince her to join my administration, at least for a while. She would be a great conduit with the alumni, and her professional experience could be a real asset.* Recalling that she had written her dissertation on development and that believed she could help the university in this area, I thought she would be a tremendous addition. Not long after she retired, I invited Evans to join my leadership team as a special assistant to the chancellor with the specific portfolio of development.

John Smith and Jeanette Evans were seasoned leaders who had many years of experience in making decisions and dealing with people. They both also had very strong moral compasses set to values consistent with my own—hard work, honesty, and a strong desire to see the university succeed. They were both examples and guides to the other members of my leadership team.

These two early appointments in building my own leadership team had served to strengthen the team through helping to communicate a clearer vision of our leadership, values, work ethic, and expectations. As a Christian leader, I believed that the best leaders were those who were reverent and possessed personal integrity. John and Jeanette demonstrated them both! Over the course of my career in leadership, I was especially pleased when new team members came with these attributes.

Establishing a Shared Vision

When I arrived at ECSU in the fall of 1995, the university sat under a pall, a kind of siege mentality that made everyone from the outside seem like "the enemy." Many people believed that the UNC system president had forced out the chancellor whom I was replacing. This chancellor was the first graduate of the university to serve as its chancellor and, for many of the alumni, this had been a particular point of pride. Supporters and members of the university community also felt they were under attack from the local newspaper. Even the *Raleigh News and Observer*, with its statewide circulation, seemed to delight in publishing stories that cast the university in a negative light. They reported on the criticisms and findings of the university's annual state audits, its bottom-of-the-system graduation rates, a declining enrollment trend, and the alleged "racist" declarations of the chancellor, among other things. And, as I have found in many communities hosting an HBCU, there were persistent rumors about its being merged with a majority-White university or changing its name to something less identifiable with its historic purpose of educating recently freed slaves and their progeny.

All of this was mixed together to create a cloud of suspicion and mistrust that overshadowed my arrival at the university. The president who sent me there to serve as interim chancellor was the same one who was thought to have forced their first *alumnus* chancellor to resign! *If Burnim is acceptable to the president and the powers that be, then he will likely not be a fervent and outspoken advocate for the university, some seemed to think.* One proud *alumna* pointedly declared, "I love Elizabeth City State and I'll do whatever is necessary to protect it. I'll be watching you!" From the outset, therefore, it was very clear that my assignment to lead this university while a search for a permanent chancellor was being conducted would be a considerable challenge, given the real issues the university faced and the suspicions emanating from the circumstances that brought me there.

My first thought was to establish clear goals for my leadership. What would I seek to lead the university to accomplish? This was a natural first step for me because throughout my life I had always framed my activities in terms of making progress toward some specific goal. In fourth grade, when

I took a math test, my goal was to make the highest grade. In high school football, when I called a play, it was with the intent and expectation of scoring a touchdown. When I went to graduate school, it was to earn a PhD so that I could become a college professor and live happily ever after. In February every year, as hints of spring started to emerge, I would always eagerly seize the opportunity to hit some golf balls to work on my game so that it would be sharp when I went on my annual March golf trip with my golf buddies, Carey Hughley and Ralph Fennell.

When I came into leadership positions at universities, therefore, my first inclination was to frame my job in terms of a goal. In assuming the chief academic officer position at NCCU, for example, I intended to lead the academic division in support of the chancellor's leadership, so that the heart of the university was aligned with the direction and speed of his flagship. "Mickey, I want this university to really value students and put them first in everything," he had told me. Hence, I translated that to the faculty and division staff so that they could easily relate it to their everyday activities. We needed to involve students in decision-making and use our best judgment and experience to serve their best interests. "Let's make sure that the Student Government Association has representatives on all our curriculum and planning committees," I declared. "Also, let's require that all faculty members participate in the course evaluation process every semester and for every class." This approach moved the campus, even if just a little, toward a more student-centric culture. My goal of supporting the NCCU chancellor's leadership became the vision that I communicated to those that I led. In effect, my goal-setting for the organizations that I led became the vehicle by which we created shared visions for their progress. I had learned that influencing people to do what they would not have done otherwise, or to go where they would not have gone otherwise, is the essence of leadership, and this is done through the creation and communication of vision for the organization.

In studying successful leaders, I had learned that this approach was one of their signature characteristics. Nehemiah, the Jewish leader in the Bible, wanted Jerusalem's wall to be rebuilt so that the Jews would no longer be in disgrace. The Reverend Dr. Martin Luther King Jr. envisioned a society where justice would apply to all and everyone would be free. Michael Jordan, considered by many to be the greatest basketball player in history, foresaw a dominant Chicago Bulls basketball team in which each member wanted to be a champion and each worked as hard as he could in practice and competition. President John F. Kennedy believed that the United States could be the first nation to put a man on the moon. As demonstrated by those people, effective leaders visualize and articulate the goal for their followers.

How could I allay the fears and overcome the suspicions of the university's constituents and supporters? And how could I simultaneously partner with them in charting a mutually-acceptable direction for the university? I sensed that the university was unclear about where it was headed or how it was going to get there. Facing these questions, I resolved to let my work speak for me.

"What are the most critical challenges and opportunities facing the university?"

"How should they be rank ordered?"

I posed variations of these questions to the members of the search committees interviewing me, to the university system head and governing board members, to the faculty members assembled at my open presentation to the campuses, and to the cabinet members. Subsequently, I used this general approach when assuming leadership of universities, boards, and other organizations that I was privileged to lead.

"Let's re-examine our strategic plan to make sure it still reflects our current reality and goals," I suggested. We quickly agreed on the historic mission described in the plan. ECSU is an HBCU, founded during our country's period of de jure segregation for the education of freed slaves and their progeny. We had a much harder time agreeing on how to articulate the current mission of the university. Everyone understood that receiving state funds obligated the university to accept all qualified North Carolina citizens, and the university had done so throughout its 104-year history. The Consent Decree between the University of North Carolina system and the US Department of Health, Education, and Welfare, however, had placed great pressure on all of the system's HBCUs to aggressively recruit White students so as to further diversify their enrollments. To many of the university's constituents and supporters, this was a clear and present danger to its identity if not its very existence! Increasing White enrollment percentages would mean decreasing Black enrollment percentages and the dilution of its Afrocentric culture, focus, and mission. Would ECSU be able to continue to emphasize the roles and contributions of Black people in our society? Would it still be able to provide the nurturing personal and intellectual growth experiences that had been the institution's hallmark?

Many feared that it would become less and less sensitive and responsive to the educational, social, and civic needs of African Americans in the region and thus destroy the institution that so many remembered and loved from years past. Unlike some fears, this one was quite rational because of the history of racism that is at the core of this country and that had been so virulent in North Carolina.

"How can we continue serving the university's historic mission and simultaneously fulfill our broader obligation to all citizens of this region and state?" I asked, trying to focus supporters on the possibilities rather than the problems. With this overarching question framing the discussion, we began to honestly explore our own reality. Gradually, we came to a mutual understanding that building the enrollment, improving retention rates, and raising graduation rates were critical existential factors for the university. Rightly or wrongly, the political climate was such that if we didn't show "progress" in those areas, it would be very difficult to maintain continued support from the state's governor and general assembly, and that was critical since the state appropriated more than half of our annual budget. In addition, the US Department of Education was already discussing ways of linking federal funding, which was also a significant part of the budget, to performance indicators.

Graduation rates were the measures drawing the most attention. Retention and progression rates were important because of their causal effect on graduation. These measures were the dominant themes for HBCUs during the 1990s and first two decades of the 2000s. During this period, the federal government pushed colleges and universities to show that they were fulfilling their missions and, by inference, that federal dollars going to them were well spent. America's institutions of higher education tended to define themselves in broad, esoteric terms for creating "educated people," or "well-rounded citizens," or "persons who can think critically, value diversity, and be productive citizens." Such concepts were not easily measured. How do you know if a person is well-rounded or can think critically? The difficulty of measuring effectiveness for higher education institutions led more and more to the use of the more quantifiable concept of graduation rates. If colleges and universities were achieving these lofty goals and indicating success in individual cases by the awarding of degrees, then one measure of their effectiveness would be the number of degrees awarded and the percentage of admitted students who ultimately completed their degrees within a reasonable period of time. Hence, graduation rates, as measured by the percentage of full-time students who graduated within six calendar years, became a de facto measure of institutional success.

After a year, the national search for a chancellor had been completed and I was selected for the job. Some skeptics remained, but those who were convinced by my interim leadership that first year outnumbered them. The work that we had done that year would now begin to yield results. During my installation address, I spoke directly about the shared vision that we had developed. When answering the question of how I planned to lead Elizabeth City State University in preparing leaders for the next millennium, I gave the following response:

> With God's help, and that of all of you, I intend to follow the strategic plan, which we developed between January and August, collaboratively with our constituents—employees, students, community and educational leaders.
>
> I envision ECSU becoming, in five to seven years, a university of 3,000 to 3,500 students who want a good education and are willing to work hard and study to earn it. I also see a university of rich cultural diversity, much as it has now, but with much greater involvement and participation in the affairs and activities of the institution by persons from those various groups. I envision a strong faculty, which is dedicated to the proposition that every one of our students is a potential Nelson Mandela, Margaret Thatcher, John Hope Franklin, Maya Angelou, (Congresswoman) Barbara Jordan, or Jim Hunt, and is committed to inspire and nurture them to develop that potential. I see a university with a baccalaureate curriculum that is second to none; one which exposes students to new ideas, teaches them to think critically,

how to recognize and appreciate differences, and how to adapt to change; a curriculum which also includes a limited number of master's degrees; offerings which extend beyond the traditional delivery methods and take full advantage of our two-way voice/video teleconferencing facility. This university will be one which is efficient and fiscally responsible, routinely gets clean audits, and which has a strong bias towards high quality service for students.

The universities that I led all had graduation rates that were below the average for all colleges and universities. For all public four-year institutions, the six-year graduation rate has hovered around 62 percent. For colleges and universities with student profiles like those I led, the same rate was usually between 40 and 50 percent. The student profiles in question include those from lower socioeconomic backgrounds, large percentages of families that have not had anyone attend college before, and students who have not been well-prepared by the public schools. These facts cause the graduation rate disparity and are the basis for myself and others to argue that simple graduation rates are unfair and inappropriate. Nevertheless, it remains an often-cited effectiveness measure and, hence, a priority for attention at institutions like those that I have served. A part of my vision has always been to help students, employees, and alumni of these colleges and universities to understand the importance of improving the graduation rates, and that real progress is possible! Hence, I repeatedly included reinforcing messages in my speeches and meetings with the various constituent groups, saying, "The goal is for all of our students to graduate in four years!" After a while, it was gratifying to hear student leaders repeat those graduation rates challenges and affirmations in their leadership activities. One poignant example would happen years later at a student rally at the state capitol in Annapolis, Maryland. The president of the Student Government Association at Bowie State University (where I was then serving as president), proclaimed, "And we will graduate in four years!" Her declaration made me smile, and feel grateful that my message was getting through and that the vision was indeed being embraced by students.

Similarly, the faculty and staff senates signaled their buy-in for the vision by supporting revisions to the university's strategic plan, which made its priority explicit—contributing to scholarship funds that would enable a larger percentage of our students to pursue their degrees without having to work so many hours to pay their expenses—and deliberately considering how their assumptions and practices were affecting the university's graduation rate. As a result, the staff at one institution devised a more hands-on academic advising process, the faculty at another reduced the general education requirements for degree programs, and the alumni at the universities increased their rates of giving and the dollar amounts of giving! These changes led to increased retention and graduation rates. A shared vision is a key to success!

Senator Basnight

Early one Monday morning, my intercom buzzed. When I answered it, my executive assistant said, "Chancellor, there's a Bill Wright on the line who says that Senator Basnight told him to call you."

"Ok, I'll take it," I responded. "Hello," I said, when connected.

"Hello, Chancellor. My state senator, Marc Basnight, told me to call you about a job."

Immediately, I imagined red flags waving vividly and felt my body starting to tense up. "What kind of job are you looking for?" I asked.

"Oh, I can do pretty much anything. I noticed that you have an opening for director of facilities."

"Yes, we do. Have you submitted an application?"

"No, I haven't."

"Well, that should be your first step. Submit your application by the deadline so it can go through the process. We'll give it very careful consideration."

This was the first time that I had received a call like this, but I sensed that it was leading me into a political mine field. I was not sure how to deal with it and decided to consult with a great university supporter and friend, who was also a master politician—Fred Yates. I told him about the phone call from Mr. Wright and asked him if he thought Senator Basnight really intended for me to hire him. "I don't know but I'll check with him and get back to you," he said.

Yates was the Mayor of Winfall, North Carolina. It was just a small township in northeastern North Carolina but Yates had managed to leverage that political base into a very powerful and influential platform in the Democratic Party of North Carolina. Over the years, he had earned the trust and support of Senator Marc Basnight and was known to deliver messages for him from time to time. Yates was in his mid-sixties, about six foot one, and still had the bearing of the marine that he had been decades earlier. I don't think he had a college degree, but as an African American man in the US South he had developed a lot of political acumen that he translated into valued service for the people of his community and region.

A few days later, my executive assistant ushered Yates into my office. His customary broad smile elicited a similar genuine one from me.

"Good morning, Chancellor!" he called.

"Good morning, Mr. Mayor," I responded. "It's good to see you! Have a seat." I directed him to the sitting area.

Rather than sitting, though, he walked over to the expanse of windows that lined the exterior wall of my third-floor office and took in the view.

"What did you learn?" I inquired.

"Marc did send that fella to you and he wants you to hire him. The guy needs a job; Marc promised to get him one, and he expects you to give him a job."

I had expected this confirmation . . . and dreaded it!

During my years at ECSU, Marc Basnight was my state senator representing all of northeastern North Carolina. More than that, he was the president pro tempore of the North Carolina State Senate and, in that role, was considered by many to be the most powerful legislator in the state. In his late fifties and with only a few community college credits beyond high school, he had risen to lead the state senate, the higher of the two legislative bodies, determining who served on what committees and setting the legislative agenda. When I came to ECSU in 1995, he had already served as a state senator for eleven years and as president pro tempore for two years. Any significant piece of legislation passed only with his approval and blessing. The entire UNC system budget, including any individual projects like a new building or professional school, had to first garner his support to have any chance of being funded by the general assembly. Hence, I had to take his "request" very seriously. I alerted the personnel department director to be on the lookout for the application.

When the application arrived on campus, the personnel director dutifully brought it to me for my review. Wright's application revealed that he had no formal education beyond high school, nor had he had any experience directly related to overseeing a physical plant like that of the university.

Oh, my, I thought. *This is a problem. There is no way we can hire this man.* I had learned earlier in my career that sometimes simply granting an interview can be a great pressure-reliever in stressful employment situations. Doing so is evidence that the candidate has been considered seriously. Hence, we invited him for an interview even though I knew we couldn't hire him.

When Wright was shown into my office for his interview, I stood and met him halfway between the door and my desk. He was wearing a button-down blue shirt with the top button undone, and what looked like a suit jacket and khaki pants—popular dress-up attire for beach dwellers on the Outer Banks.

Shaking his hand, I directed him to one of the two armchairs directly facing the desk. I then walked back around the desk to my leather executive chair. After we exchanged pleasantries, I asked him to tell me more about his experience. "What have you done that would prepare you to be director of facilities?"

"Well, I've been a boat builder for most of my adult life," he said. "I've made sailboats and, I must admit, they are about the best you can get. That's what I've done and that's what I know."

"Is there anything else that we should take into account as we go through this process?"

"No, just that Senator Basnight sent me to you, and I really believe that I could do the job."

Interviewing an applicant who had not been advanced through the process was unusual, but justified in light of the senator's interest in the case. After Wright's interview, however, I told the director of personnel to proceed with the search and hiring process as normal, which meant that the vice chancellor to whom the facilities director would report would make the final hiring decision. Unsuccessful candidates would be notified that their applications had not been advanced.

After those notices went out, Senator Basnight called me directly. "Mickey, I sent you word that I wanted you to hire Bill Wright," he told me, clearly agitated. "He's a good man and he needs a job." My heartbeat sped up and I even thought I could hear it beating in my chest.

"Yes, senator, I received your message and, as a result, I interviewed Mr. Wright myself. He is not qualified for the facilities director position and we couldn't hire him. The position had been advertised publicly, across the state, and specific minimum qualifications were listed in those ads. I didn't think that you would want it known that you had advocated for the hiring of an unqualified individual in violation of state and federal laws."

At that he seemed to be a little less agitated and we ended the call. I didn't know what consequences I would have to face, but was thankful that God had given me the strength to take the right position.

A day or two later, Yates told me that he had heard about my call from the senator. "He respects you for standing up to him," he said. I also sensed a hint of admiration from Yates. After this episode, he and I remained on friendly terms, as did Senator Basnight and I.

This experience had reinforced the notion that doing the right thing would not always be easy, but that approach to leadership is the one that left me feeling best about myself, regardless of the consequences.

The Leadership Development Institute

Elizabeth City State University was a remarkable university in rural eastern North Carolina. With an enrollment of around 2,000 students, it was the smallest university in the University of North Carolina system. The faculty took great pride in teaching students from challenged educational backgrounds and of limited economic means. The staff embraced a student support culture that compelled them to be proactive in routinely helping students overcome obstacles to success. For example, admissions counselors would befriend their recruits and serve as internal advocates in helping them find financial assistance even two or three years after their initial enrollment. In another instance, I saw a staff member introduce a student to an alumna from the Washington, DC, area so that she might get a ride home since she didn't have money for a bus ticket. A student-centered service mentality goes a long way in fostering student success. I came to believe that this culture emanated, in part, from similar experiences and backgrounds of many of the faculty and staff. As I recall, about twenty-five percent of the staff were from eastern North Carolina and graduates of the university. This was a benefit because it enabled them to easily identify with ECSU students, but it also led to the challenge of limited exposure to new ideas, approaches, and ways of doing things. Hence, some staff members found their upward mobility at the university was hindered when new positions were created. As I sought to lead the university toward a new vision and a greater level of success, I needed people who were committed to student success but who also understood and embraced change as a catalyst for progress. How could I take advantage of the existing student-centered service culture and put employees in a better position for personal growth so that the university could continue to progress?

My thinking about building and sustaining successful organizations had been influenced by some of the popular leadership literature of the day, including Jim Collins' *Good to Great*,[3] John Maxwell's *The 21 Irrefutable Laws of Leadership*,[4] and Noel M. Tichy's *The Leadership Engine*.[5] Tichy's words especially resonated in my mind: "The winning leaders I have met all view teaching as one of their major jobs, and they spend a lot of time doing it. . . . The real essence of leadership is assessing changing situations and motivating others to act in an appropriate manner."⁶ After looking at CEOs like Jack Welch of General Electric, Andy Grove of Intel, and Roger Enrico of PepsiCo, Tichy concluded that "leaders must draw appropriate lessons from their experience and then take their tacit knowledge and make it explicit to others."⁷

Aha, I thought. *That's the answer to my question!*

At my next Wednesday morning cabinet meeting, I queried my direct reports. "What do you think about my starting an institute to enhance the leadership potential of university employees?" I asked. "It would be for faculty and staff, and anyone in a leadership position or who aspires to a leadership position."

"Why do we need an institute?" the vice chancellor for business asked. "We already have degree programs that employees can take if they want to enhance their leadership knowledge and skills."

"Yes, that's true. But we need something less formal and of shorter duration so that people can quickly focus on what they need to know to be more in sync with today's university and where we're headed. The world has changed and the university needs to change also. People need to understand that and know how they can participate in and facilitate this change!"

"What would be the curriculum and who would teach it?" my director of public relations and marketing asked.

"I would be the teacher and I would focus on my brand of leadership," I said. "My goal would be to show them how I make decisions—ones that are in the best interest of the institution and are consistent with our values—and equip them to come up with their own answers and approaches to problems. The curriculum would include analytical problem-solving, building self-respect and confidence enhancing the workplace environment, the essence of leadership, ECSU's values, mission, and vision, and how to give feedback."

"How would participants be selected?" the director of HR asked.

"I want there to be some status associated with participation," I responded, "so persons who wanted to be part of the institute would submit simple applications, which I would review, and then send letters to those accepted. The applications process would only be used to limit the cohorts to no more than twenty persons and assure a good cross-section of employees, considering the four divisions of the university, jobs, and gender."

Dr. Evans, our distinguished alumna and leading donor, asked, "When would the classes meet? And how often?"

"Well, I've thought about that. I know people will likely get more out of the experience if they have some investment in it, and since there is no monetary tuition or fee, I figured it might work to have them sacrifice some of their time. I'm thinking about scheduling the institute sessions one Saturday morning each month for six months. That way, students would have to give up some of their precious free time in order to participate. People willing to do that would have some investment in their participation. What do you guys think?"

"That's good! It could work," Evans responded. "I think this Leadership Development Institute would be a great vehicle for professional growth for our people and you should go forward with it." Several other cabinet members nodded or spoke in agreement. The skepticism of a couple of them, however, was revealed by their silence and noncommittal body language. Though the idea had been mine, I too was nervous about its prospects for success. But we needed to do something to enhance the university's brand and grow its enrollment!

"That settles it then. I'll send out a memo describing the institute, announcing that we will start it this fall, and inviting people who are interested to apply."

I spent the summer thinking about the institute and planning it to incorporate the content and techniques that I wanted to provide to participants. Of the twenty-one applications submitted, ten employees were selected to be in the first cohort.

The first meeting was at nine o'clock on Saturday morning, September 28, 2002. I made a point to get there by 8:30 a.m. to meet the caterers, arrange the seats in a semicircle, and make sure the handouts were ready. As people trickled in, speaking to each other politely and getting coffee, tea, and breakfast pastries, I sensed some uneasiness in the room. They had followed my suggestion to dress comfortably casual and I was glad to see that no one had interpreted that as license to come in cutoff jeans or sweatsuits more appropriate for painting or exercise workouts. The participants were present and ready to begin, but I could see that they were uncomfortable in the presence of each other. There were a couple of deans, an accounting clerk, an HR professional, a residence hall manager, and a couple of maintenance workers in the group. This kind of gathering was very unusual and the participants weren't sure what to expect. In the normal course of business, employees from the various university jobs would have little opportunity to interact with each other in a setting like this. Faculty members usually talked to and worked with other faculty. Similarly, housekeeping staff, accounting staff, admissions staff, and others tended to interact primarily with their close colleagues. How was this going to work?

I led this first session in a manner that would become the pattern for all the institute classes. We followed a detailed class schedule, which I had carefully prepared to assure that we would cover the specific objectives that I had set for that class meeting. Our first thirty minutes were spent doing a "get acquainted" exercise. The participants were given five minutes to get to know another member of the class. Afterwards, each participant was given one minute to introduce this person to the class. This icebreaker exercise helped the class members feel more at ease and set a collegial tone for the institute sessions. Next, I spent brief blocks of time explaining the necessity for the university to change to meet the evolving needs of our students and community—our changing world, the purpose and goals of the institute, and my expectations for them as participants. Following that, I led them in a very deliberate discussion of our institutional priorities, shared vision, and institutional values, which are foundational for all my decisions and actions as chancellor of the university.

Following a break, our next agenda item was "Who is Mickey L. Burnim?" In this twenty-minute segment, I shared some of my own background—rural, humble beginnings, Christian values, belief in pursuing excellence in everything I do, and lastly tying that in to the specific institute objectives:

- To sharpen participants' understanding of ECSU's mission, priorities, vision, and values;
- To help participants understand that every problem is an opportunity and that every opportunity can be approached from a number of different ways; and
- To give participants greater insight into Mickey L. Burnim, the chancellor!

Knowing that students learn more as active participants rather than passive ones, I wanted the institute sessions to have a high degree of individual involvement—not one where students could come, sit quietly, and take notes without saying anything or being engaged. Therefore, as a pedagogical device for these sessions, I chose to use case studies. To do this, I wrote brief descriptions of university issues or problems, highlighting the decision to be made or the actions needed.

"Any similarities to real people or situations are purely coincidental," I told them tongue-in-cheek. Following is one of these case studies.

Case: "A Disgruntled Worker?"

Mr. M. Ploy Yee has worked for the university for eight years. He has received one promotion during that period, but feels very much underappreciated. He feels that he should have been promoted at least to assistant vice chancellor by now. He knows that he could do the job better than his boss who now holds that position. In fact, he feels that his boss is moving their unit backwards. He firmly believes that the way they did their work before his boss came was better than what they're doing now. Mr. Yee knows that the new procedures will not work, so he's just waiting for his boss to fail. Then they'll see that he was right all along.

As his supervisor, you have observed a sullen, uncooperative attitude in Mr. Yee. He begrudgingly does just what is asked of him and nothing more. He makes a point of saying that certain functions are not part of his job description and that his work day is from 8:00 a.m. until 5:00 p.m. Overall, you have been able to decipher his thoughts and feelings through his offhand remarks, conversations with other workers, and reports from some of those other workers.

What issues are relevant in this case? What are the facts? What are Mr. Yee's feelings? Is change involved? If so, how? Is Mr. Yee's motivation a problem? What, if anything, will you do? Why?

After dividing the class into three or four groups, I distributed the case statements to each group member. Usually, I gave each group a different case to analyze, but sometimes gave two groups the same case.

"You have fifteen minutes to analyze the case as a group and decide your answers to the questions. I want each person to be involved because I may call on any member of the group to share the group's responses and explain how they were derived."

This was done to guard against some persons fading into the background of their groups and not participating. Everyone had incentive to be involved! As they engaged in their group analysis, I walked around the classroom and observed their interactions. I looked for broad levels of participation and different perspectives because of the diversity of jobs and university divisions represented.

At the conclusion of the fifteen-minute group work period, I tried to foster learning by creating spirited and challenging discussion by asking questions.

- "Mr. Wilkins: what are the facts of the case?"
- "Ms. Lewis: Describe Mr. Yee's motivation issue. How did your group decide to address it? "
- "Dr. Blackmon: your group had the same case. How did you decide to address Mr. Yee's motivation issue?"
- "Group C: Which response to Mr. Yee seems best to you? Why? What important principles or values are in play?

These cases were designed to foster discussion among the institute participants and provide an opportunity for me to demonstrate how I approach problem-solving. Hence, after facilitating their lively discussion of the cases, I would tell them what I saw and how I would address the case.

"As I see it, the central issue in this case is Mr. Yee's attitude. Because he feels underappreciated, he is giving less than his best at work. So the relevant question is, how to assure him that he is valued and help him see why it's important that he give 100 percent. Some might ask, 'How can we motivate him?' I believe, however, that motivation must come from the inside. I can explain the advantages of giving one's best—raises, promotions, recognition—as well as the consequences of not giving one's best—mediocre-to-poor evaluations, smaller salary increases, being passed over for promotions—but Mr. Yee will have to decide to give his best. Explaining the consequences will need to be done sincerely and sensitively, but the decision will have to be his!"

While sharing my thinking about the case, I tried to read the faces of the participants and could see the lightbulbs of understanding being switched on. I hoped they saw that I would strive for clarity with sensitivity. Institute evaluations from the participants showed that they loved discussing the cases and that they were learning how to be better leaders at the university.

At the end of the first institute class meeting, I assigned two books for the class to read as preparation for future discussion and application in case analyses. They were Spencer Johnson's *Who Moved My Cheese?* and *Fish* by Stephen C. Lundin, John Christensen, and Harry Paul. These short and nonintimidating volumes conveyed an air of fun in delivering their powerful messages, and served as the primary texts for the institute.

Did this institute actually work in developing leaders inside the university? Well, more than eighty employees went through it during the three years that we ran it with only a couple failing to complete it. Persons completing it were given a certificate of completion and priority consideration for promotions, and a number of them actually rose in the campus leadership ranks.

One day a couple of years after starting the institute, three of the "graduates" scheduled a meeting with me to talk about the institute. I was caught totally off guard, having no idea why they wanted to meet with me. The leader of this delegation was Derrick Wilkins, the director of academic computing. "Chancellor Burnim," he said, "several of us who were in the first LDI cohort were talking recently about how much we enjoyed those Saturday morning sessions and would love to meet with and discuss cases with our campus colleagues again. So we've come to ask you to consider having a some kind of reunion for us—an LDI refresher!"

At that moment I felt a deep sense of satisfaction and gratitude. My idea of enhancing the internal leadership potential for the university by facilitating the development and growth of ECSU employees was working and was appreciated! After I had left, Derrick Wilkins went on to earn a doctoral degree and rose to become chief of staff to the chancellor. Several other graduates of the institute also received new jobs and promotions within the university. To God be the glory for the things he has done!

A Leadership Dilemma

"Mickey, we need to speak to you privately for a moment."

Walter Davenport, the chair of the board of trustees, pulled me aside, along with two other members of the board and a student, to join him in the my office. This was the morning of the board meeting and my staff and I were busy attending to last-minute details for the meeting that would take place that afternoon. Something was up and I had no idea what it was. What did the chair of the board and other trustees need to say to me this morning? Had I violated some protocol? Or failed to inform them about something important happening on the campus? Since he had also called a student leader into the meeting, I wondered if she had raised some student issue with the chair before mentioning it to me.

As the three of us gathered in my office, Mr. Davenport did not wait for us to sit down before he began to talk. "Danita, tell the chancellor what you told me," he said to the student leader.

"Two days ago," Danita said, "Dr. Searcy called and asked me to come to her office. During our meeting, she told me that she had learned from people in the president's office that you would soon be removed from the chancellorship and that she would be named acting chancellor. She wanted my support as a student leader."

Searcy was a senior vice chancellor whom we had hired for another position two or three years earlier. She was subsequently chosen to fill the current position when its occupant moved on to another university.

"Had Dr. Searcy told you about this?" Davenport asked me.

"No, she hadn't," I said.

"I didn't think so. She's disloyal, and I felt you needed to know."

This board meeting was taking place on the heels of my receiving word that the current president of the system was out to get me and I had better watch my back. I had scheduled a meeting with her to discuss the rumors, but we had not yet met. I felt as if I had been sucker-punched and all of the wind had gone out of me. Why had Searcy not at least given me a heads-up? These board members seemed to think that her failure to do so implied her complicity in the removal plot. Without saying so, they seemed to want me to take some action against her.

I was not sure what to do. I believed the student leader was telling the truth. Yes, I was very angry with Searcy for not showing me the courtesy of telling me what she had been told, even though I suspected that she had been asked not to share it. Just as she had chosen to tell the student leader, she could've alerted me, the chancellor who had hired and promoted her, about the plot. All of that aside, we had a trustee board meeting to get through. We followed our established schedule and navigated their agenda with the usual efficiency. But that pre-meeting discussion weighed heavily on my mind!

Loyalty was not a litmus test for being on my leadership team, even though it was expected. I certainly felt an obligation to show loyalty to team members. This lack of loyalty hurt me deeply and I knew that I could no longer trust Searcy. I wanted to confront her with what I knew, but did not want to put the student leader in a vulnerable position. If I was removed and she became acting chancellor, then the student could be subject to some kind of punitive action. Instead, I decided I would revoke Searcy's access to my online calendar. She had requested this access as a means of making it easier for her to do her job in supporting my work as chancellor, so I knew it was important to her. I did not take this action to be vindictive, but as a defensive step. Revoking her access would put her outside my inner circle and let her know that I was unhappy with her, but not jeopardize the student. Hence, I opened my computer desktop, went into the calendar settings, and removed her name as one who could access my calendar!

In less than two days, Searcy noticed that her access to my calendar had been removed and she called. "Mickey, I attempted to place a meeting on your calendar and received a message that I did not have access. Did you know about this?"

"Yes, I knew. In fact, I removed your access."

"Why did you do that?"

"I had good reason."

"Well doing so limits my effectiveness."

I realized that I had acted too quickly. I would either have to tell her I knew about her disloyalty and that it had eroded my trust in her, thereby exposing the student leader, or restore her access to my calendar. I couldn't take the chance of putting the student in a vulnerable position, so I restored her access. I would just have to manage continuing to work with a senior vice chancellor whom I couldn't trust until I found out what was really going on with the system president. Of course, I prayed about this situation and felt led to trust God and let him work out this situation for me. I was not to be vengeful or try to take matters into my own hands.

This situation demonstrated that sometimes your most trusted team member will be disloyal and maybe even seek to undermine your leadership. Even matters like this require careful deliberation and thoughtful consideration of any possible consequences of your actions. Who is likely to be affected and how will the organization be affected?

Books: To Rent or Buy?

"What do you mean 'book rental system?'"

Provost Searcy had just informed the cabinet that she and the academic deans were recommending that the university end its book rental system. Having never heard of a college or university book rental system, I was incredulous.

The provost was a mathematician who stood about five foot nine and spoke with the certainty and authority of a drill sergeant barking precise orders to a group of new recruits. She had come to ECSU a few years earlier as a dean and was elevated to provost when that position became vacant.

"You heard me right," she responded. "All of our students are charged a $315 rental fee for textbooks, which entitles them to pick up all of the books for their classes from the campus book store at the beginning of the semester and return them after the class ends."

At this point, from my position at the head of the conference table, I turned to face Jean Sims, my executive assistant, who sat to my immediate right. "Ms. Sims, you've been here longer than any of the rest of us. What's the story on this rental system?"

"We've had this system in place for many years. It has been an important part of the university's strategy to keep the financial burden of attending college as low as possible, and we calculated that it saves our students between $200 and $400 per year."

"We understand that," the provost chimed in, "but the deans and I believe that this system has a number of negative impacts that outweigh the monetary savings. First, under the rental system, our faculty is required to use whichever textbook edition they choose for their classes for at least two years. This means that, in some cases, textbooks being used are outdated and don't reflect the current state of knowledge in the discipline."

"Second," she continued, "the faculty feels that by renting books to students, we are communicating a message that owning books is not important when, in fact, we believe that the building of a personal professional library should be considered an investment in intellectual capital that will pay dividends throughout one's life."

I sensed that those around the table who had been regular faculty members sympathized with this sentiment. "Well, what do you think?" I asked the cabinet.

"Students will not be happy with this change!" offered the vice chancellor for student affairs. "So we can expect them to oppose it vigorously."

"If we make this change," offered the vice chancellor for business and finance, "we could commit to providing financial aid refunds to students on the first day of classes so students can purchase their books as soon as possible. We could also work to keep the markup on textbooks in the bookstore as low as we can." He spoke with the quiet assurance and competence that stemmed from his years of experience in the UNC system and commitment to our leadership team's success.

We continued to discuss the matter for a while and, finally, I thanked the cabinet members for their active and candid participation. "I'll weigh your comments carefully and make my decision so that if I decide to go with the policy change, we'll be in a position to present it to the board of trustees at its next meeting."

After mulling it over for a couple of days, I met with the provost. "I'm not convinced that eliminating the book rental system would be best for our students. I agree that having a personal library is important but I don't believe that all students would be better off buying their books, especially since many of their required texts are not in their major fields and they would only end up reselling them to the book store for pennies on the dollar."

"Mickey, you can't go against the faculty on this," she said. "They strongly support eliminating the rental system and you need to support them on important matters like this."

I was still not convinced, but the provost's argument struck a responsive chord in me. My relationship with the faculty was good, but tense. I had been at the helm of ECSU for nine years and had the battle scars to bear witness. During that time, I had been criticized for reaching out to the local community to try to build stronger support from local business and civic leaders, some of whom faculty, staff, and alumni considered enemies of the university. We had taken a hard line in restricting the freedom that some faculty members had become accustomed to as we worked to improve the security of our campus IT infrastructure. We had also not been able to raise faculty members' salaries as fast or as high as they deserved, and we had participated in system-wide budget cuts when forced to by economic conditions or action of the North Carolina general assembly. Going through each of these episodes caused me to lose two or three more supporters, and I was always on the lookout for ways to gain more support among the university's constituent groups, especially the faculty. Hence, I decided to move forward with the proposal to replace the university's book rental system with a more traditional purchase system.

The Board Meeting

My staff and I followed our usual process of preparing a proposed agenda for the approaching board of trustees meeting and we included on it the replacement of the book rental system. I began to draft a letter to the university's students, to be distributed after the board meeting, explaining the policy shift. In that draft, I explained how the university's administrative council, the campus' highest policy-approving body, which included student members, had approved the proposed change. I told them that building a personal professional library was an investment in intellectual capital that would pay dividends throughout their careers, and that the expected additional costs would be eligible for coverage by their federal financial aid packages. The letter represented my best effort at rationalizing the policy change and convincing our students of our good intentions and their potential benefit. I didn't consider the possibility that the board would not approve the policy change, because our carefully considered and recommended policies had always been approved in the past.

The board of trustees meeting began normally in the second-floor conference room of the campus library. Trustees had come from various parts of North Carolina and Virginia and they greeted each other, my senior staff, and me with handshakes, hugs, and smiles all overlaid by the din of joyful conversation. Board members took their seats at the tables, which had been arranged to form a large rectangle. Walter

Davenport, the chair of the board, called the meeting to order. The roll call and approval of the minutes were dispensed with, and focus quickly turned to the chancellor's report.

"Mr. Chairman and members of the board," I began, "I'm pleased to recommend for your consideration and approval a book purchase policy to replace the book rental system currently in use at the university." I then recounted the arguments for the change and the campus process through which the change had been approved. I felt that I had done my job well in making the recommendation professionally and convincingly without any hint of the doubt that I felt about the new policy.

Davenport then called for a motion to approve the policy change, which was seconded immediately. "Discussion," called Davenport as he turned to look at the student trustee. This is when our plan for a smooth and uneventful meeting began to fall apart. The student trustee, who was also the president of the Student Government Association, raised his hand for recognition and then began to speak. "Students are really upset about this," he said. "Books are very expensive, and our students are already stretched too thin. We don't need to keep many of the books used for our classes, and many of us are barely scraping together enough money to get by now."

I could see the sympathetic head nods around the tables, indicating that the student's comments had struck a chord. Board member Mary Purnell then said, "Mr. Chairman, I call the question."

"The question has been called. All in favor say 'Aye.' All opposed, say 'Nay.' The nays have it and the motion fails!"

I was stunned. The board, for the first time, had rejected one of my recommendations! I felt embarrassed. I saw their vote as a personal rebuff . . . a very public statement that my judgment was flawed, and that I had given them a bad recommendation! *Would they ever trust me again? Was this the opening of the floodgates to second-guess all of my recommendations?*

This episode was a leadership failure. I felt some uneasiness about opposing the rental system from the time it was proposed and should have stuck with my gut—my first inclination. The faculty proposal was reasonable, but it really didn't put the needs of the students first. Our students were, for the most part, from very poor economic circumstances, and for them, that reality trumped almost everything else. Good servant leadership should always focus first on the greatest needs of those being served!

It was not too long after this experience that my administrative assistant buzzed me on the intercom one day and announced: "There's a Jim Appleberry on the phone for you." I took the call and was delighted to hear a greeting from an old friend. "Hello Mickey. This is Jim Appleberry. How are you?"

"I'm doing fine, Jim. It's good to hear your voice. It's been a while," I commented.

"Yes, it has. I'm working with a search firm now and we're handling the search for a new president for Wise University and one of our finalists works for you. What can you tell me about Dr. Searcy?"

Appleberry and I had been colleagues and friends for about ten years. We met over the telephone during my first or second year at ECSU when he president of the American Association of State Colleges and Universities, (AASCU). He had called to extend a personal invitation for me to join the association of state college presidents and chancellors. Moved by his gesture, I joined AASCU and thus began a twenty plus year active membership which provided great support for my leadership through its various programs and opportunities to interact with other presidents and chancellors and their partners. By calling me, he was reaching out to a colleague and friend who was in a position to give him very useful information about Dr. Searcy.

In response to his question, my gut said *Tell him that she can't be trusted and that I would not hire her again.* My head said, *Put your feeling aside and consider the question objectively. She is a strong leader with good academic instincts and she would not have to report to anyone on campus.* My heart said, *This is the right approach to take.*

"Jim, Searcy would probably be an effective president. She's smart, has a strong personality, listens to the faculty, and can make decisions," I shared. I had chosen to say the most positive things that I could while being completely truthful. Ultimately, she was hired for that presidency and, from what I know, served that university well.

BETWEEN A ROCK AND A HARD PLACE

The intercom on my desk buzzed, alerting me to a call from my executive assistant. "Yes?" I asked.

"You have a call from Dr. Joseph James."

"Ok, you can put him through," I said. "Good morning, Dr. James! How can I help you?"

"Doc, I just wanted to tell you again to watch your back. The president is out to get you!" This was the second warning that James had given me about the president of the UNC system, my boss. The first one I had dismissed, since I just couldn't make any sense of it. The president and I had had a cordial and respectful working relationship up to that point. I had been supportive of her leadership and very diligent about keeping her informed of campus and community issues—submitting reports, data, etc. according to her requests. We also had in common that we had both studied economics at the graduate level so, presumably, we tended to view the world through similar lenses. In addition, I had just completed my five-year comprehensive review, and both the consultant and the Elizabeth City State University Board of Trustees had given me a stellar assessment. In his report to the board, the external consultant had written: "Mickey L. Burnim is not only doing an excellent job as Chancellor, but he is headed in a direction that, if he continues, could lead him to be a truly outstanding Chancellor!" The board reviewed his report, accepted, and concurred with it, and included it as part of their very positive report on my leadership for that five-year period. So, it was inconceivable that the president could hold any animus toward me or have any issues with my leadership.

Yet, here I was, face to face with a second warning that the president was less than happy with my leadership. And the warning came from a member of the governing board for the university system and an alumnus of Elizabeth City State. "You can verify this by talking to Sally," he offered. Sally was another member of the board of governors, and one who was also from the eastern region of the state—ECSU's primary service area.

Sally confirmed James' story. "Yes, Mickey, you need to be really careful with her."

At this point, I decided to take matters into my own hands. I called the president and told her that I would like to come for a meeting with her.

"Yes, Mickey, that's a good idea. We should get together to talk," she said.

We set the meeting for a couple of weeks later in her office. During that interim period, I approached one of her vice presidents to see if she could shed any light on this confusing situation.

"Yes, Mickey. Ever since you refused to tell Senator Basnight that you didn't want the Pharmacy School, her attitude toward you has been markedly different," the vice president told me.

Now it was starting to make a little more sense. One day a few weeks earlier, State Senator Basnight had called me in a burst of excitement. "Mickey, how would you like to have a pharmacy school?"

"Wow, that's an interesting idea! I hadn't thought about it," I responded.

With obvious enthusiasm, the senator continued, "If ECSU had a pharmacy school, you could channel your students into it. That would be a very lucrative career option for some of them and it would help to alleviate the shortage of pharmacists in northeastern North Carolina."

"Yes, it would," I agreed, consciously trying to show real interest in the idea while cautionary alarm bells were going off in my head. My experiences with NCCU's Law School and their nursing program and ECSU's nursing program had shown me that professional schools and their rigid accreditation requirements could be a real problem for limited-resource institutions serving high percentages of economically and socially disadvantaged students. And I was pretty sure that a pharmacy school would be very expensive to operate.

"So, what do you think?" he asked me.

"Senator Basnight, a pharmacy school could be a real boon for ECSU, but only if fully funded! Our resources are already stretched thin and we simply could not justify redirecting existing funding for a pharmacy program when the ones in our inventory need more money. If we tried to launch one with no new appropriations, or with insufficient new appropriations, then it wouldn't be a quality program and would not be able to achieve accreditation."

"Mickey, don't worry about that. The general assembly will provide the funding," he assured me. Basnight was president of the North Carolina Senate and, arguably, the most powerful politician in the state.

"In that case, ECSU would be thrilled to have a pharmacy school," was my enthusiastic reply. And this apparently was the first pull of the thread that led to the unraveling of my good relationship with the UNC system president.

In retrospect, I could see that the first hint of trouble came during my obligatory call to the president to inform her of the conversation with Basnight. I didn't want to violate the "No Surprises" rule.

"What was your response to him?" she asked.

"I told him that if it were fully funded we would love to host a pharmacy school."

"Mickey, you know they're not going to fully fund it."

"I have my doubts, but didn't think it wise to tell the senator that I didn't believe what he was saying. Furthermore, if word got out that I had told Senator Basnight that I didn't want ECSU to have a pharmacy school, I would lose all credibility as ECSU chancellor and as a civic leader in the eastern North Carolina region."

We ended the conversation and, though it had not gone well, I believed that I had taken the right position.

Not long after that conversation, my executive assistant transferred James' first warning call to me, and added, "You know he applied for your job."

"What do you mean?"

"He was a candidate for the ECSU chancellor's position, and he wanted it badly, so just be aware," she warned. I filed that away and tried to focus on my regular duties and responsibilities.

One afternoon a few days later, my executive assistant said, "Dr. Lane, our band director, requested a meeting with you and I scheduled it for 3:00 p.m. today."

As Lane entered my office for our appointment, I directed him to a chair in front on my desk and I sat behind the desk. "What can I do for you?"

"Chancellor, the band has received two invitations to march in Christmas parades on the same day and I just wanted to make sure that our choice is acceptable to you," he said.

"Dr. Lane, why are you coming to me with this? It's a matter for you and your band members to decide."

"I know, but one invitation is from the town of Riptide and one is from Manteo. We went to Riptide each of the last two years and the band voted to accept Manteo's invitation this year, but I thought I'd better check with you."

Then it hit me. Riptide is a little township of a few hundred people, but its mayor is none other than Sally Baker, the board of governors member who confirmed that I had become a burr in the president's saddle! Mayor Baker would not be pleased that the band had chosen to go to Manteo, a predominantly White community, rather than her township of poor African Americans.

"Dr. Lane, you and your band should decide which invitation to accept and I will support your decision," I said.

"After going to Riptide the last two years, the students want to go to Manteo this year," he said.

"Fine," I responded, remembering that Manteo was Senator Basnight's hometown. "I'll support your decision."

He thanked me and left my office.

The next morning my administrative assistant buzzed the intercom to tell me that Mayor Baker was on the line. Picking up the phone, I chimed, "Good morning."

"Well, it would be a good morning if I hadn't gotten that call from Dr. Lane yesterday," she said. "Do you know they turned down our invitation for them to participate in our Christmas parade? They are the featured attraction and our kids so look forward to seeing them. Can't you do something?"

"Mayor Baker, when Dr. Lane brought this matter to me yesterday, I told him that the band should decide which invitation to accept and that I would support their decision. Since they had been to Riptide two years running, their going to Manteo this year seemed reasonable."

"What? You knew about this and approved their going to Manteo? How could you? I can't believe it."

"Yes, I did. Our primary service area includes all of northeastern North Carolina, including Manteo. And they had been to Riptide two years in a row."

Mayor Baker did not accept my reasoning and questioned my commitment to the economically disadvantaged northeastern North Carolina community of color. I felt emotionally drained after the call, but was determined to keep providing the best leadership that I could as I defined it—with reason, fairness, and integrity. The band performed in the Manteo Christmas parade and enjoyed the experience, but I suspected that I had not heard the last of this episode.

As the date of my meeting with the president approached, the former chair of the ECSU Board of Trustees, Charles Penny, called.

"Dr. Burnim, I ran into Ben Ruffin in Raleigh and he mentioned that the president had invited him to a meeting about you in her office. I thought I should mention it to you?"

Ben Ruffin was a member of the board of governors for the entire university system, and therefore, one of the president's bosses. He was also one of the most influential African Americans in the state. Ruffin told Penny that he understood the president had also invited some other board members to the meeting.

Why had the president invited them to our meeting, I wondered. When I talked to her to set up the meeting, I left that conversation with the impression that it would only be between us. What was she plotting?

I began to suspect a setup. The president was inviting other people to a meeting I had requested without informing me. That's when I decided it would be good to have a knowledgeable and supportive ally in the meeting also—Earl Brown, ECSU Trustee Board member.

I contacted him and asked, "Earl, can you attend a meeting that I have scheduled with the president? Charles Penny told me that she has invited some members of the board of governors, and I would like for you to be there if you can make it. I suspect that there may be an attack on my leadership and it would be good to have an ECSU Trustee Board member present to represent that board."

On the day of the meeting, I drove the 150 miles or so to the general administration building in Chapel Hill and went directly to the president's office. "Good afternoon. I have an appointment with the president," I announced to the receptionist.

"Go right in."

The president's office was small for a CEO, likely owing to the first UNC system President Bill Friday's unassuming persona. He was president when the building was constructed and the first president to occupy the office. As I recall, the office furniture included the president's desk, a couch and matching love seat, and an upholstered winged chair positioned around a coffee table. I entered the office and greeted the president and her vice president for finance, who was seated on one end of the couch and her vice president for academic affairs, who sat on the love seat. The president was probably in her early sixties, stood about five feet six inches tall, and wore high heels and expensive knit suits befitting a CEO. She had hired the vice president for academic affairs from outside the system, and the two of them were contemporaries. The system chief financial officer was about ten years younger, and had worked his way through the ranks of financial management in the system office.

I sat in the winged chair. Ruffin arrived next and sat on the loveseat. Brown walked in shortly afterwards and sat on the couch. Ruffin was a very fit sixty-something-year-old who was on a path that would lead him to become the first African American chair of the board of governors. Brown was in his fifties and serving in his second term on the board of trustees. Just as I sensed that the president was about to start the meeting, James and Baker walked in. James was a tall man, probably in his late fifties, and Baker was probably about the same age and a committed community activist. Both were recent appointees to the board of governors. The president called for her staffers to bring in two more chairs and they were plopped down with their backs in front of her desk in the only remaining floor space.

The president rolled her chair around her desk to be closer to the rest of us and began. "Well, Mickey, you know that for some time we've had concerns about your leadership at Elizabeth City." I was immediately taken aback. I could feel my heartbeat accelerate as I interrupted her.

"No, I am not aware of any concern with my leadership," I stated forcefully while trying to maintain a cool, steady demeanor. "The university has been making measurable progress toward its goals and my annual reviews and the comprehensive review were stellar! No one has said anything to me about concerns!"

The president then glanced at her vice presidents as if seeking their concurrence. They shrugged and said nothing. She continued, "Well, maybe we haven't shared our concerns with you directly." But some board members have expressed their concerns to me and I thought we needed to meet. I'll let them speak for themselves."

She then paused and looked toward James and Baker, clearly expecting them to voice their concerns. After a few moments of awkward silence, the president spoke in generalities about being unclear about my goals and how they meshed with the needs of eastern North Carolina communities, and of just what I was trying to do in leading the university. I found this comment odd since, under her leadership, my performance evaluations had been among the highest for all chancellors in the system. I don't recall any direct questions or specific concerns being raised during the meeting. Brown shared that the board of trustees was very happy with my leadership, as was reflected in their comprehensive evaluation, which had been submitted to her. Her vice presidents and Ruffin indicated that, from their perspective, my performance was at least comparable with the other chancellors in the system, and Dr. James and Mayor Baker were noticeably quiet. After a period of general conversation that seemed to me to be space-filler to try to justify the meeting, the president ended it.

"Thank you all for coming. Mickey, we'll send you a letter describing and detailing the concerns that I mentioned."

During the drive back to Elizabeth City, I reflected on the meeting and tried to figure out what it was all about. I surmised that James and Baker had been talking to the president about me and she expected them to agree with her statement about concerns and express their own in the meeting. I'm not sure why they chose not to speak. Maybe the president had misinterpreted comments they might have made to her about my leadership. Baker later told me, "I do have issues with your leadership, particularly your decision to let your band go to Manteo instead of Riptide, but I would not allow myself to be used as a tool to bring a Black leader down. So I remained quiet in the meeting."

I don't know, maybe James felt the same way. It's also possible that neither wanted to be transparent about their conversations with the president. Neither of these scenarios explains what caused her to change her attitude about my leadership. I suspect that the change stemmed from my refusal to tell Basnight that I didn't want the pharmacy program at ECSU. Whatever the case, I knew that it was in God's hands and I had left that meeting with my job intact and no delineation of specific areas of concern regarding my leadership. I would await her follow-up letter.

About ten days later, the promised follow-up letter appeared in the stack of mail that my executive assistant had screened before placing it on my desk. "Mickey, my leadership team and I are not sure just what your broad goals are with respect to university-community relations," the letter stated. "We want to know more about your plans and strategies." I decided to treat the letter as a legitimate expression of their concerns rather than an ex post facto rationale for calling a meeting in the first place.

Essentially, I responded to the president with: "My intent is to promote and project Elizabeth City State University as 'the university of northeastern North Carolina.' Hence, our marketing, student recruitment, and donor-cultivation initiatives and activities are all geared toward that outcome. We want the vast majority of the people of that region to see the university as an asset enriching the quality of their lives."

"That is helpful. We'll follow up in the future," was her response. I never heard anything else about the matter.

With my agreement, Basnight moved forward with his advocacy for a pharmacy school at ECSU and sponsored funding legislation in the North Carolina state senate. To my knowledge, neither the president nor any member of her staff ever expressed any public opposition to the project. In fact, at the direction of the president's office, we collaborated with the University of North Carolina at Chapel Hill to plan and establish an extension of their school of pharmacy at ECSU. All involved agreed that this would be the most reasonable way to move toward developing a stand-alone pharmacy school for ECSU. I think it is fair to say that our colleagues at UNC Chapel Hill were not thrilled about the project, but felt that active opposition to an initiative being championed by Senator Basnight would be unwise. The president's office and the UNC Chapel Hill administration worked with us to include funding for a pharmacy building and state-of-the-art technology for instruction. Students applied to the UNC School of Pharmacy for matriculation at ECSU. The pharmacy classes at ECSU were technology-based and relied heavily on state-of-the-art, real-time, interactive voice and video communications. A couple of years later, the president "retired" from the presidency and, not long after that, I moved on to become president of Bowie State University (BSU) in Maryland.

This experience illustrates an important reality for leaders: a smooth-sailing ship can suddenly encounter rough seas! A good captain will try to anticipate and prepare for such beforehand, but often cannot. Some just can't be forecasted. My approach was to always try to be truthful and direct. I tried to always do the right thing!

Transitioning from ECSU to BSU

This "Between a Rock and a Hard Place" experience had really shaken me to my core. At the very time that I had felt most validated by the comprehensive chancellor's review process, including an external reviewer's evaluation, I had learned about an undercurrent of doubt and dissatisfaction emanating from the university system president's office. More than just unappreciated, I felt like I was under attack. The hurtful rumors were more than that. The president really did have some concerns about my leadership and obviously had been in some discussions about it with at least two members of the system board of governors, though not with me. I felt compelled to deal with the real possibility that my leadership at ECSU would be coming to an end. I needed to update my exit plan and prepare for the next chapter in my life.

In December of 2005, I updated my exit plan.

A Plan for Exit from the Chancellorship and Retirement

> September 2008—Announce retirement from chancellorship for June 30, 2009
> June 30, 2009—Retire from ECSU chancellorship with fourteen years of service
> July 1, 2009 —Begin year of retooling for teaching and research
> August 2010—Begin teaching and research at ECSU
> June 30, 2011—Retire from ECSU/State of NC with thirty years of service (including a year's worth of unused sick leave)

This was the map that I wanted to follow, as it was the shortest path to retirement in North Carolina with full benefits. I knew that I might have to change this plan in response to action by the president or others, but was not too bothered by this possibility since she had already announced that she would be retiring in 2006. Even so, I still believed that having an exit plan was a good idea. I had enjoyed the privilege of leading ECSU but was beginning to feel the toll of its stresses and strain. This particular leadership season was coming to an end.

One day not long after I completed this update of my exit plan, my secretary put through a call to my office. "Hello, Dr. Burnim. This is Marion Frenche with Greenwood & Associates and we're handling the search to find a new president for Bowie State University. Were you aware of their search?"

"Yes, Ms. Frenche. Dr. Lowe is a colleague in our athletic conference and he had informed us that he was leaving."

"Well, your name was given to us as a good prospect and I'm calling to see if you are interested."

"This is a surprise to me, Ms. Frenche, and I'm not sure."

"What would it take to make you interested?"

"Well, if you told me that you've researched my background and believe that Bowie State needs someone like me, and the governing board is looking for someone like me, that would peak my interest."

"I haven't researched your record, but I will do so and get back to you."

Three or four days later, Frenche called back and said, "Dr. Burnim, I have looked at your background and reviewed your record and believe that you are just the kind of person that Bowie State needs and is seeking!"

I found her report easy to believe because I had also done my research by visiting the BSU website and reading about the university's history, organization, and statement about the search, and had reached the same conclusion. I thought, *Even though I'm not looking for a job, this looks like it would be a great fit and opportunity to finish out my higher education leadership career.*

"Well, Ms. Frenche," I said, "in that case, you can enter my name into the search process."

Bowie State's enrollment was about 5,000 students—roughly twice that of Elizabeth City State. It is in a metropolitan setting as opposed to ECSU's rural setting. Also, whereas ECSU sits in an economically depressed part of North Carolina, BSU is located in the Maryland county with the highest income per capita for African Americans in the United States! ECSU's academic program inventory was almost exclusively at the undergraduate level, offering baccalaureate degrees and three master's programs by the time I left. Bowie State, on the other hand, offered a broad array of master's-level programs along with its extensive baccalaureate inventory, and even a doctorate in education. Both were HBCUs, but they were clearly very different institutions.

About a week after allowing my name to go forward, Frenche called me directly and announced, "Dr. Burnim, you have been selected as one of the semifinalists in the Bowie State presidential search."

I was happy to learn this, but not really surprised. I thought that my background, higher education experience, and leadership success at ECSU made me a great match for what BSU needed at that time. This is when I allowed myself to start thinking about extending my career beyond my current planned retirement in 2011 and leading Bowie State University as its president. This could be a new opportunity in a different place with new challenges.

The BSU Interview Process

As one of the seven semifinalists, I was invited to Maryland for an airport interview. The first interview in a presidential search was referred to this way because it typically took place at a location near the airport to minimize the possibility of compromising the search by prematurely revealing candidates being advanced in the process. "The search committee has scheduled a meeting with each semifinalist to size them up and decide who they wanted to invite for campus interviews later," Frenche told me. "A reservation has been made for you at the Sheraton Hotel near the airport."

"Thank you. I'm looking forward to it."

I flew into the Baltimore/Washington International Thurgood Marshall Airport the night before the scheduled interview. It was to be held in one of the hotel conference rooms and I timed my arrival to be five minutes before it was to begin. As I entered the conference room, a tall, trim man with dark skin, a well-groomed mustache, and freshly cut salt-and-pepper hair stood from his seat at the head of the elongated conference table and extended his right hand. "I'm William Missouri, the chair of the search committee," he said. "Welcome!"

I had been told that he was the administrative judge for the Circuit Court of Prince George's County. "Good morning, Judge Missouri. Thank you. I'm delighted to be here," I responded as I shook his hand.

After our exchange, I turned to introduce myself to a person standing near him who was looking directly at me, then willingly glided into a kind of impromptu waltz that took me around the room to introduce myself and shake hands with every person present. As I neared the end of this opening dance, Missouri directed me to take the seat directly opposite him at the other end of the table.

"That's the hot seat!" one of the men joked. I smiled and sat as directed.

Now facing Missouri at the other end of the table, I saw that he had the bearing of a distinguished elder. He really looked like the leader of this group! Calling the gathering to order, Missouri announced, "Even though he has just met us all individually, I want us to go around the room and tell him again who we are and which university constituency we represent."

There were four faculty members, including Dr. Joan Langdon, a professor of computer science who had worked at the university for many years, and Dr. LaTanya Brown, a young economics faculty member who had just come to the university. Also included were the presidents of the Student Government Association and the Graduate Student Association, two staff members including Cynthia Coleman, chair of the Staff Council, Attorney Orlan Johnson from the University System of Maryland Board of Regents, Dr. John Wolfe, liaison to the office of the chancellor, Jan Greenwood, president of the firm that was assisting with the search, McKinley Hayward, president of the BSU National Alumni Association, and five business and civic leaders including Mike Little, a member of the BSU Foundation Board, and the person who had made the "hot seat" comment earlier.

After the introductions, Missouri announced, "Dr. Burnim, if you would like to, we've allocated five minutes for you to give an opening statement. After that the committee members have some questions they want to ask you." I was prepared for this. This was my fourth interview with a search committee for a university CEO position so I had a good feel for the kind of questions they would likely ask:

"Why are you interested in this position?"
"What makes you well qualified for this position?"
"What is your educational philosophy?"
"What is your leadership style?"
"What does shared governance mean to you?"
"What are your strengths?"
"What are your weaknesses?"

In fact, I had written out those likely questions, carefully crafted my answers to them, and rehearsed giving those answers. Additionally, I had led a campus for eleven years and felt confident that I could draw upon my experiences to respond plausibly to any question they might ask.

I had also anticipated the opportunity to make an introductory statement and chose to use it to paint a picture of just who I was. In preparing my interview notes, I wrote "Who am I?" and answered with: "Economist (social scientist); husband, father, grandfather, brother, and son."

For "What are my values?" I noted "Integrity, collegiality, teamwork, competence, respect. I am a Christian and I try to live by the Judeo-Christian ethic of 'Do unto others as you would have them do unto you!' I would never try to force my beliefs on anyone else but want you to know how I approach people and situations."

As the interview progressed, I felt that my responses were on point and showed the confidence of an experienced campus CEO. God was clearly in control and this process would go according to his will. The head nods and smiles from faculty members on the committee left me with the impression that I had won their support and I believed that was key. The committee interview had gone well and I started to feel the tension release that I always experience after a successful speech or public appearance!

As people were leaving the room, Jan Greenwood came over to me and asked, "Mickey, can I talk to you?"

As the president of the search firm that was assisting Bowie State, Greenwood had a vested interest in the success of the process. Since they had reached out to me late in the process, I sensed that the search committee was not satisfied with the number of very competitive candidates who had emerged to this point. She wanted me to be a very strong candidate because this would make her firm look good! We walked out of the room together and she commented: "I thought you did well in the interview, but you need to tone down the religion!"

"Thanks Jan. I hear what you're saying." I hadn't anticipated this reaction from her, but I understood it. Religion is a sensitive topic and evokes different reactions from different people. In fact, it can be a red flag for many, and so voluntarily interjecting it into an interview for a job at a secular institution is fraught with danger. Of course, I knew and considered that as I prepared for the interview and chose to take the risk because I really wanted the committee to know who they were getting if they chose me. The fit between the university and the president must be a good one to work best for the institution and I wanted to be clear about who I was. Besides, I didn't feel it was quite the risk that Jan thought because I knew that my belief system would resonate well with most of the people in the room.

Meeting the Chancellor

The next morning, I was to meet with the head of the University System of Maryland, Chancellor Brit Kirwan. Bowie State is in that system, and the presidents of all of its constituent institutions report to him, including the president of Bowie State. We had agreed to meet in the hotel restaurant. I timed the trip from my fourth floor hotel room to the restaurant so that I arrived right at our 8:00 a.m. meeting time. Though it was only about half full, the restaurant was bustling as waiters and busboys moved about and some customers made their way through the buffet line. I looked around the restaurant and spotted a white-haired Caucasian man sitting alone at a table who was looking toward the entrance to the restaurant as if he were expecting someone. Our eyes met and I took a couple of steps towards his table. He smiled, stood up and said, "Hello, Dr. Burnim?"

"Yes."

"I'm Brit Kirwan," he said, and he extended his hand to shake mine. He was about six foot one inch tall and flashed a very genuine and engaging smile that made me feel like he really was glad to see me. We sat at the table for a few minutes exchanging pleasantries and then went through the breakfast buffet line to get our food.

"Mickey, thanks for meeting with me and for applying for the BSU presidency," he said when we returned to the table. "You have a very impressive curriculum vitae and are a very strong candidate."

"Thank you," I said. "I've been blessed."

"The university has a lot of potential that it hasn't yet tapped into. There is great opportunity for enrollment growth and fundraising."

"That's good to hear!"

"But it also has a serious impediment to its progress. The Faculty Senate doesn't seem to understand its role in the governance of the institution and regularly tries to overreach!"

"Oh . . . what do you mean by that?"

"Well, instead of focusing on curricula issues and academic policy, they often intrude into the administration of the institution. Not too long ago, the Faculty Senate chair came to my office to complain that the BSU administration had bought a pickup truck and hadn't conferred with them before doing so!"

"What? That's clearly the responsibility of the campus administration!"

"Yes, that's right. As I'm sure you can see, this approach fosters a very contentious relationship between the Faculty Senate and the administration, which makes it nearly impossible for them to collaborate for the advancement of the university."

"Brit, I've found that Faculty Senates can be challenging at any institution but that honest, collegial, and transparent leadership can make for a positive relationship over time."

"Yes, I've found that to be true as well. But the BSU Faculty Senate chair, James Jones, is a special case. Whoever the next president is will very likely find a formidable foe in him."

"Well, Brit, if I were selected as BSU's president, I would begin with an open mind and a clean slate. I would assume that everyone had the best interests of the university at heart and would be amenable to working collaboratively through transparent and honest dialogue toward the progress of the university."

"Mickey, that's an admirable way to start, but what if that assumption is proven false?"

"I assure you that I have the strength and resolve to do what needs to be done for the good of the university."

"It's good to hear that. I've enjoyed getting to know you. The search committee is moving along pretty quickly now so you'll hear from them very soon. Thanks again for coming."

THE CAMPUS VISIT

Things were indeed moving quickly at this point of the BSU presidential search. The university's representatives had been in the latter stages of the search when Frenche had contacted me, so much of the candidate vetting and reference checking had already been completed for other candidates, which is likely why my candidacy advanced so rapidly. A few days after my interviews, Frenche notified me that I was one of three finalists the search committee had decided to invite for campus visits, and they asked me to bring my wife. I was thrilled and excited to receive this news, since it confirmed that my candidacy was very strong and that the chance of my being selected had improved to one in three! In fact, as I thought about LaVera accompanying me on the visit, I felt the quiet, calm assurance that the campus visit would lock the position up for me!

LaVera is my deal-closer, I thought. Being almost six feet tall, with a natural smile that automatically spreads across her face when she meets new people, and body language that communicates an air of self-confidence, LaVera commands attention when she enters a room. Her choices of costume jewelry and conservative but stylish clothing, similar to but less expensive than St. John knit suits, revealed her practicality and good taste, and complimented her stature in a way that put people at ease and evoked admiration. Yes, the search committee would like her and easily visualize her as a great first lady, and they would ascribe some of her attractiveness to me! Case closed! Deal over!

"Babe, I've been selected as one of the three finalists for the BSU presidency and we've been invited to visit the campus!" I told LaVera excitedly.

She smiled. "That's great! I expected them to invite you to campus."

"I know they will love you when they meet you and that will make all the difference!" I exclaimed.

"I'm not going," she stated calmly.

An expression of shock and panic must have overtaken my face as I cried out. "What? Why not? They asked me to bring you!"

"You have applied for the job, not me! They are hiring a president, and it's the presidential candidate who should go for the campus interviews. I don't like the implication that I automatically come along as part of a package deal to perform some undefined, uncompensated but expected role."

I was stunned. I hadn't anticipated this response. I knew that her sincerity and honesty often led to unfiltered directness in her communications, but I hadn't taken the time to consider this from her perspective. "Dear, you are right! That's exactly what they are doing and it is unfair! They're applying an old-school model of a university president with supportive wife who represents the president and the university with grace and effectiveness, with little recognition and no compensation!"

"Yes, you've got it!"

"I understand your perspective and it is more than justified. When you think about it, though, that's exactly what we have done here at Elizabeth City State! And we have done it extraordinarily well! This is an opportunity for us to go to Bowie State and serve students, alumni, and citizens in a new place and make an even bigger difference. Even though they are making some unjustified assumptions and unfair expectations, this is an opportunity for us to do what we do on a bigger stage! I would really like for you to reconsider and go with me for the campus visit."

We had both seen what a big difference college educations had made in our own families through her older siblings and my parents, and we both had a strong desire to help create similar opportunities for other families. I thought it might help my case to remind her of this.

She sat silently for what seemed like several minutes, but must have been only a few moments. "Ok," she said, "I'll do it for you."

On the day of our campus visit, at 6:15 a.m., a black Ford LTD pulled under the covered driveway at the front of our airport hotel to pick us up. Recognizing it as the car that we had been told would be sent for us, LaVera and I immediately walked toward the front doors. As we crossed the threshold, the car's driver greeted us in a resonant baritone voice: "Dr. and Mrs. Burnim? Good morning; I'm Nathan Long and I'm your driver for the day." His comforting voice, paired with the genuine smile on his face, provided a very warm greeting for us on this important morning.

"Good morning, Mr. Long. Thank you for picking us up this morning," I replied as he opened the rear passenger door of the car and we slid into the back seat. "Do you work for the university?" I asked him.

"Yes, I've worked in the university's transportation department for almost twenty years. I'm glad to have drawn the assignment to transport you from the hotel to the campus today."

In short order, we were on the Baltimore-Washington Parkway heading toward Washington, DC. This part of the ride was very scenic, with lush green trees lining both sides of the four-lane highway, and the natural grasses, shrubs, and trees of the median separating the lanes. Along the route, we also saw segments of a low rock wall that looked like remnants of the Depression-era Public Works Administration or a Civilian Conservation Corps project. I learned later that the parkway was constructed in the 1950s and that the rock wall segments were decorative overpass and ditch barriers.

"Mr. Long," I asked, "how is it to work at the university?"

"Dr. Burnim, it's a great place to work," he said. "I've really enjoyed it!"

"Oh? What makes it such a great place to work?"

"Well, I like the variety of people that I get to drive around—other staff, faculty, and students. I also really like going to their various activities like ball games, meetings on other college campuses, and even meetings or field trips in DC. It's always interesting."

After a while, Long turned off the parkway and onto a narrow two-lane paved road that turned out to be Maryland Highway 197. This felt like a drive in the country, as we drove along the curved road, up and down the hills, and through a forest for about five miles. This sure didn't feel or look like an urban or cosmopolitan area. We had passed through no housing developments or commercial areas. I knew that we were between Washington, DC, and Baltimore, but couldn't see or feel any connection. In fact, up to this point, it looked even more rural than Elizabeth City!

"Mr. Long: I'm surprised that the trip to campus is so dominated by rural scenery. Where's the development?" I asked.

He chuckled and agreed. "You're right Dr. Burnim. This route makes it look like Bowie State is in the country. But if you continue on this road past the campus, you'll pass through a lot of housing developments, strip malls and town centers, schools, gas stations, and so forth. It's not nearly as rural as it looks."

Without warning, the forest ended and we made a left turn into what a sign announced was Bowie State University. It was 6:55 a.m., five minutes before our scheduled arrival time.

We were met on campus by four members of the search committee. They introduced LaVera to a couple of student leaders who would give her a golf cart tour of the campus, and then escorted me to the Rathskeller in the student union for a breakfast meeting with the president's direct reports, deans, and assistant/associate vice presidents. The breakfast meeting was scheduled from 7:30 until 8:30 a.m., and even though this wasn't an interview, I knew that I would be watched very closely throughout the day. I knew that I would feel some level of stress, but determined that I would bear it as best I could.

The first meeting after breakfast was with the faculty. The convener for this meeting was Dr. Fred Mills, one of the faculty representatives on the search committee. Calling the session to order, he began, "Dr. Burnim: you have up to ten minutes to highlight your qualifications and your reason for interest in the presidency of BSU. The remaining hour and five minutes will consist of dialog and questions and answers."

I used the ten minutes to give a shortened version of my introductory statement to the search committee during my first interview, being careful to emphasize the thoughts, experiences, and qualifications that would be of greatest interest to that constituent group. For the academic administrators with whom I had breakfast, I talked about my leadership style of delegating with clear instructions and mutually agreed upon objectives and timelines, and my high expectations for excellent performance. In my session with the nonacademic staff, I emphasized how critical I believe they are to the overall success of the university, and described how I had encouraged the establishment of a staff senate at ECSU. Alumni are always interested in how receptive a president will be to their perspectives, and so I described a desire for their input on matters of importance to the university.

Of all the "discussion" sessions on my schedule for the day, this one with the faculty gave me the greatest angst. It was held in the large lecture hall in the education building because the committee anticipated that a lot of faculty members would want to attend. The lecture hall was tiered so that, after entering from the back, one had to descend about fifty steps to get to the lectern on the four-inch-high stage at the front. Standing there, I could see that the hall was about three-fourths full, with most of the faculty sitting in the middle section and fewer seated outside the two isles. This session had a very different feel from the others that day because it was in a much larger venue and had a lot more people in attendance. I felt like I was under a microscope, and I was!

As I made my introductory remarks, I could see that their eyes were focused directly on me and some even turned their heads to one side so as to hear me better. They were listening intently—not just hearing what I was saying, but trying to read between my lines, making inferences and drawing conclusions. By nature and by academic training, faculty tend to be skeptical and critical, and I didn't want to say anything that would needlessly cause any of them to oppose my candidacy. I knew that the faculty voice was the most critical one in this process.

The questions seemed to get easier as the session went along, likely because I could draw upon my nine years of experience as a university provost and eleven years as a chancellor. So with each question and response, I gained confidence and became more at ease . . . until a man near the back of the center section raised his hand for recognition and then asked, "Dr. Burnim, what are your thoughts about the pending decision from the Office for Civil Rights?"

The wheels in my head started turning. *What was he talking about? Was this some widely publicized, widely known issue that I missed somehow?*

"Sir, I'm not familiar with what you're referring to. What is it?" I responded truthfully.

"The state of Maryland and the Office for Civil Rights in the US Department of Education entered a partnership in 1999 for the purposes of improving the educational opportunities for African Americans in Maryland's public institutions of higher education and ensuring compliance with the state's obligations under federal law. Maryland's report was filed and we're waiting on OCR's assessment. Do you think Maryland is in compliance with its obligations under federal law?"[8]

I now understood. This was a question intended to lead to insight about my views on the federal government's treatment of HBCUs and how aggressive an advocate for full compliance I might be.

"Thank you for that clarification! I understand the importance of your question but must admit that I don't know the particulars of the Maryland OCR case. Hence, I really can't comment on it directly. I note, however, that I was very much involved with the North Carolina case. I testified as an expert witness before a federal judge on the importance of the HBCUs and, later, when I worked in the UNC system office, actually helped to implement the North Carolina commitment to strengthen its HBCUs and enhance educational outcomes for African Americans. I am committed to seeing that the state of Maryland follows the law in working to increase African American students' access, retention, and graduation rates in Maryland."

I hoped my response would suggest a reasoned, determined, and persistent approach that was an accurate reflection of my personality and style. The questioner sat back in his chair as if mulling over my response, but did not ask a follow up. The next question was on a different topic and the rest of the faculty session was uneventful. As I left this meeting with the faculty, I exhaled, releasing a good bit of the tension that I had felt throughout the session and thought, *OK, Mick. You've gotten through the toughest test of the day.*

This was the first in a series of "discussions" with various constituent groups of the university that would be held that day. They had been planned to last an hour and fifteen minutes each and were intended to allow the university's constituencies to see and hear the finalists. Each session was convened by a member of the search committee whose job was to manage the time, keep notes to share with the committee when they got back together, and listen to specific feedback from the constituents after the session.

I met with staff, alumni, friends, community representatives, students, and others for discussion sessions that went on until time for dinner with the search committee at 7:00 p.m. The day was almost over and I felt that I had done a good job. At least I had not committed any serious mistakes and had made good impressions with most of the people who had participated in the day's sessions. All that remained was to get through dinner. I knew that my social graces were still being measured to gain insight into how I would represent the university in public, but to me this was a matter of being rather than doing. Besides, LaVera was with me and I knew that her friendly and unassuming manner would go a long way toward winning them over for Team Burnim!

Meeting with the Board

The next morning I met with the board of regents for the University System of Maryland, the governing board for Bowie State and the other eleven universities in the system. This body held all legal authority for each of the twelve public universities that comprised the University System of Maryland and, collectively, they would make the decision as to who would become the next president of Bowie State University. As I was ushered into the conference room at the system office, I saw that it was packed with most of the seventeen board members crowded around the long oval-shaped wood conference table.

"Dr. Burnim, please take the seat at the head of the table," Board Chair David Nevins directed. The room was not very wide, so the seated board members had to scoot in toward the table for me to walk past to get to my chair. While taking my seat, I noticed that most of the board members were White males with a couple of women. Attorney Orlan Johnson, who had served on the search committee, was the only African American member present.

As I recall, the questions asked by board members were general and philosophical. For example, "How do you see the relationship between the president and the governing board?"

"I believe that the best arrangement is when the president and the board work as partners in providing leadership for the university. The board sets policy in accordance with the mission of the institution and lets the president lead and operate in a manner consistent with those policies, and keep the board well informed about the most important happenings at the university," I replied. Satisfied looks and nods around the table confirmed that I had struck a responsive chord.

Toward the end of the session, Nevins asked, "Do you have any questions for the board?"

"Thank you. Yes, I do," I slowly breathed out as I thought about my conversation with Chancellor Kirwan about the faculty leader who was 'a special case.' "If selected for this position, I intend to work very hard at shared governance in a spirit of genuine collegiality, but there may come a time when I will need to make a tough personnel decision given what I've been told about the challenging antagonistic relationship between past presidents and the Faculty Senate leadership. What kind of support can the new president expect from this board?"

As soon as I got the words out of my mouth, Chancellor Kirwan, who was not a member of the board, spoke up: "You would have unbelievable support from the board!"

I assumed that he was speaking from his experience in interacting with members of the board during times when other presidents were facing difficult challenges from this particular faculty member or others. It was reassuring to hear members of the board speak up to voice their support for the president.

From my perspective, the meeting with the board of regents went well. I felt I had allowed my experience to shine through as well as my strength and determination. Working as a team, LaVera and I had done our best to advance my candidacy. Though it had been very intense, we felt good about our visit with the university constituents and the board as we returned home to Elizabeth City, and were ready to accept whatever outcome came.

New Opportunities, New Challenges

Early one morning about a week after our visit to Bowie, my personal cell phone vibrated in my pocket and played its melody to notify me of a call. "Hello," I answered.

"Good morning, Mickey. This is Brit Kirwan. How are you?"

"I'm doing fine, Brit. How are you this morning?"

"Just fine. I'm calling to tell you that the board has chosen you to be the next president of Bowie State University!"

I felt a satisfying smile spread across my face and my heart beat a little faster with excitement. We had done it! By the grace of God, our territory was being expanded and we were going to BSU to face new challenges and lead it to greater levels of success in serving its students, community, and the whole state of Maryland!

In my exuberance, I had no inkling of the degree to which this new assignment would test my faith and shake me to my core.

Following a brief negotiation process, I happily accepted the offer to become the next president of Bowie State University and a date was set to hold a press conference to announce my selection to the public. On the day of the press conference, LaVera and I happened to be in Washington, DC, participating in the American Association of State Colleges and Universities' (AASCU's) Millennium Leadership Institute, so the trip to the BSU campus was a much shorter one than we had had to travel from Elizabeth City, North Carolina.

We rode to campus in a chauffeured town car that the university had provided. When we arrived on campus, I recall that we were greeted by Kirwan, Board member Orlan Johnson, and outgoing president Dr. Calvin Lowe. They escorted us to the large lecture hall in the education building where I had met with the faculty a few weeks before. Kirwan began the meeting: "As you know, several months ago, Lowe announced his intention to resign from his position as president of Bowie State University to pursue other interests, and I, subsequently, appointed a search committee to conduct a national search to find a new president. That committee has completed its work and I am pleased to announce today that the board of regents has elected Dr. Mickey L. Burnim to be the next president of Bowie State University!"

There was polite applause and Kirwan went on to highlight my twenty-four years of higher education leadership including my successful tenure as chancellor of ECSU, where we established a strong working relationship with faculty, increased community collaborations and involvement with the university, grew the enrollment, and ramped-up institutional fundraising. He introduced LaVera and then invited me to the stage to make a statement and answer questions.

As I took the stage, I could see fifty to seventy-five people scattered throughout the lecture hall with some reporters and camera persons up front. I was well aware that this was my only chance to make a good first impression on the faculty, staff, students, and community members who were present, but I felt a sense of calm self-assuredness that was very different from the nervousness I felt when I stood in the same spot before the faculty a couple of weeks earlier.

"Good afternoon!" I began. "I'm delighted to greet you as the newly elected president of Bowie State University, and I must thank the search committee, Chancellor Kirwan, and the board of regents for giving me this wonderful opportunity! I look forward to working with all of the university's constituents, especially the Student Government Association, the Faculty Senate, and the Staff Council, in helping the university to reach its full potential. My administration will be one characterized by transparency through frequent and open communications."

I believed that this approach would be very effective at a university that had seen a lot of distrust and internal strife and I was determined to tell people what to expect so they would be more likely to see and appreciate it as it unfolded.

After answering a few questions, I returned to my seat. As I did so, President Lowe stood and took the stage. "Dr. Burnim, would you join me?" President Lowe was about six feet tall, a man of considerable girth and an ever-present, easygoing smile. I returned to the stage and stood beside him wondering, *What's he doing?* Out of the corner of my eye, I caught a glimpse of Chancellor Kirwan's face, which mirrored a quizzical smile. That's when I noticed that he was holding something in his hand.

"Mickey, you and I have known each other and served together on the CIAA Board of Directors for several years and I was pleased to hear that you would be my successor," he said. "I want to pass this lapel pin on to you as a symbol of my well wishes for your season of leadership at Bowie State." It was a small, gold-colored bulldog with tiny red jewels for eyes. The bulldog is BSU's mascot. His expression of support simultaneously humbled and buoyed me.

I began serving as Bowie State University's ninth president on September 1, 2006, when the university was in the midst of gearing up for a new school year. As usual, there was a lot of activity on campus at this time of the year—students were completing the registration process, faculty were finalizing preparations to teach their classes, the administration was working on its budget request for the next year, and the campus-shared governance units were preparing for and conducting their first meetings for the new year.

Ever since my initial meeting with Kirwan, my strategy was to be deliberate and direct in communicating and working with the Faculty Senate to try to establish a genuine sense of shared governance that was consistent with generally accepted definitions of "shared governance." I remained keenly aware of the task of building positive constructive relationships with the faculty, particularly its leadership. Hence, I invited Faculty

Senate Chair Dr. James Jones to my office during my first week at the university to further foster a spirit of goodwill and cooperation. Jones is about five feet seven inches tall, with a squat physique and a permanent gruff facial expression. His stout appearance hints at the role of head football coach that he held decades earlier, but he now operated as a professor of sport management.

We sat in the sitting room in my office. I sat in the upholstered armchair facing the door to my administrative assistant's office, and he sat on the couch against the wall to my left. Early during our meeting, though, he sat on the edge of the couch and looked me directly in the eye.

"I want you to know that I personally led votes of 'No Confidence' in the last three presidents."

If he hadn't already had my attention, that statement would have gotten it. I interpreted it as a warning. He wanted to be clear that if he were dissatisfied with my leadership, he would call for the faculty to vote "No Confidence" in me! Since the faculty has no authority to hire or fire a president, such a vote is the strongest expression of disapproval that the collective body can make and it often brings a presidency to an end.

"Well, that's an interesting revelation," I noted. "I think you will find that my leadership at Bowie State will be consistent with my record at Elizabeth City State and what I've promised to do here."

At the first Faculty Senate meeting, just three weeks after I arrived, I had my first chance to speak to this representative body of faculty members and I wanted to get off on a good foot in establishing a positive working relationship with them. I wanted them to know that I valued them, wanted their input on matters important to the university, and wanted them to hear my assessment of the challenges and opportunities facing the university at that time, and how I intended to lead.

The Faculty Senate met in the second-floor conference room of the campus library. Tables were arranged to form a large square with a speaker's podium at the far end of the room. The senators, persons representing all of the academic departments, sat on all sides of the square with the officers sitting on the side opposite the podium. As I walked into the conference room, I was greeted warmly and shown to a vacant chair next to the officers.

After determining that a quorum was present, Jones called the meeting to order and led the body through the roll call and approval of the minutes from the last meeting. Then he welcomed me on behalf of the senate and invited me to speak to the group.

I thanked him, told the senate how glad I was to be with them, and began: "We have an opportunity to overcome Bowie State's reputation." I wanted them to know that I had already learned BSU was known for great strife between faculty and the administration. Several of the community and civic leaders who had served on the search committee shared this with me after my selection and this reinforced what Kirwan had told me.

"I want to work with you for the benefit of the university. My focus really is on making the university as strong as possible for the effective service of the students." This was my way of saying "Let's stop the in-fighting and work together to advance the university!"

I went on to point out how I was following through on my promised commitment to shared governance with the appointment of faculty members to the communications task force, the strategic planning committee, and several search committees for vice presidents. My strategy was to tell them what I wanted them to see, knowing that my actions would speak louder than my words.

The first year and a half went well. I attended the meetings of the shared governance groups, gave updates, and answered their questions regularly. In a unified effort, we were able to focus on building the university's leadership team, increasing enrollment, and creating our fund-raising infrastructure. We were consistent in honoring and communicating with our shared governance partners, and these efforts paid off. In his first year-end performance evaluation letter to me, Kirwan wrote:

> Perhaps, the biggest challenge you faced was the campus environment and culture, which had grown extremely negative and contentious. Amazingly, you have completely turned this situation around, so much so that I received several letters from members of the faculty supporting your leadership, including letters from individuals who have been long-time critics of the BSU administration. You made a promise to the campus to have an "open" administration and to set a tone that was respectful of diverse views. You have clearly delivered on this promise and, as a result, there is the most cohesive and supportive spirit at BSU that I can ever recall. This is a remarkable achievement, one that results from your personal values and exceptional administrative skills.

Who had written letters of support for me to Kirwan? And why had they done so? As far as I knew, this was not part of the annual performance evaluation process.

"Mrs. Ward, do you know about these letters that were sent to the chancellor?" I asked Denise Ward, my administrative assistant.

"Yes," she said, "I called several faculty and staff members around the campus and asked them to write letters of support for you to the chancellor."

"Why did you do that?"

"I know that Bowie State has a reputation for being divided and fighting internally, and thought that the chancellor needed to hear firsthand what a positive difference you have made. And you know I'm on assignment!"

Ward is a unique individual with an unforgettable personality. A quiet woman in her mid-forties, she was known around campus as a humble person and a devout Christian. She routinely shared Bible scriptures that were on her mind, or a recording of a song or a sermon that she had heard and was quick to encourage anyone who she sensed needed it. After coming to work in the office of the president, it didn't take her long to tell me that she was "on assignment from the Lord to support my ministry of leadership." So, after she reminded me of her "assignment," I didn't ask her any more questions about the letters!

One of the letters was sent by Jones, chair of the Faculty Senate! Like the others, it was effusive in its praise.

> "This has truly been an enjoyable and productive year. In fact, I never dreamed Bowie State University could find such a dynamic leader (sic) . . . His relationships with the faculty have been congenial, constructive, and cooperative. Deeply and broadly concerned about the dignity and the rights and the opportunity for fulfillment of all human beings, he has infused new and richer dimensions of energy and enthusiasm into all of our relationships."

I felt deeply humbled by these testimonials and prayed: "Thank you, Father, for using me to bless this university and its constituents through my leadership!" Maybe changing the culture at Bowie State University wouldn't be so hard after all!

It was my first cabinet meeting and I slowly turned my head to make eye contact with each of my eight or so direct reports seated around the circular conference table. Present were all the people who reported directly to me—the vice presidents, chief of staff, clerical staff, director of marketing and university relations, and director of athletics. Their expressions were mostly blank with just a hint of excitement. I began by saying:

> "Ladies and Gentlemen, I assume that you know your jobs very well and are willing to perform them at a very high level on a continuing basis. I aim to do my very best every day in pursuing the mission of this university—expanding opportunities for people to get an excellent education, all while creating and maintaining an environment where people enjoy learning and working, and where they are treated with dignity and respect. I'm counting on all of you to join me in this effort."

I believed that in the absence of massive dysfunction, transformational change was more effective when done gradually rather than abruptly. In general, human beings are resistant to change and a gradual approach can make the change more palatable and give those affected more time to adjust. Hence, I wanted them to know that they would have time and a reasonable chance to prove themselves.

Then I paused to cast another deliberate glance around the table, and saw in their faces confirmation of a lesson I had learned years earlier—that my words alone would not do much to assuage the uneasiness that often accompanies a new leader, but I intended to follow up with actions that reinforced this message and I believed that most of them would meet my expectations.

There were a couple of exceptions. The vice presidency for student affairs was being filled on an interim basis and I quickly began the process to find a permanent vice president. Secondly, I had never worked in a setting with a chief of staff, and having this position did not mesh well with my preferred organizational structure, which favored a strong provost. Hence, I notified the chief of staff that I would be eliminating his position and asked if he might be interested in something else at the university. He showed no surprise and seemed to take my notice in stride. For me, personnel decisions were always the hardest to deal with because they have a direct impact on a person's livelihood, and sometimes reputation, self-image, and career path. It always helped a little bit to remind myself that my first obligation was to the university. Hence, I tried to do what was best for the university while attempting to treat individuals with dignity, respect, and compassion. In these instances, this meant applying the Golden Rule of "Do unto others as you would have them do unto you!" In this case, the chief of staff's reaction made it easier. "No, I think it's time for me to move on," was his retort. His decision was better for the university's budget, since I would not have to find another position for him at the university.

After a few months, I started to have serious concerns about whether the provost that I had inherited was the best fit for my leadership team. In one of our earliest conversations, I had said to her, "I have no doubt that you have what it takes to be an excellent provost and I want you to succeed on my team." But it seemed that her ambition for becoming a president herself was keeping her from focusing on her job of provost. Having gotten a taste of presidential leadership from serving as interim president for a month after I was named, but before I assumed the role, she was not going to be happy with any other position. She applied for numerous presidencies over many months and was selected as a finalist for several of them, but was not successful in them. I sensed that her primary goal of becoming a president and the disappointment and frustration of not being selected for one in that first year-and-a-half prevented her from giving her best effort as provost at Bowie State, and I had to address that issue. She was a seasoned college administrator, having worked in various capacities at two or three other institutions, so she knew what a what a top-level administrative position required.

"Rita, I'm not convinced that you want to be part of my team," I told her. "You're not responding to Blackberry calls, email messages, or voicemail messages, not responding in a timely or comprehensive way even after I call things to your attention, and you're missing deadlines."

Her countenance usually revealed an easy going manner, but her expression now appeared to be one of resignation, acceptance of the truth of my observation. "Your attitude is not one of cooperation and enthusiastic mutual support," I continued, "and you are not maintaining the same pace as the rest of the team." These were some of the things that I had told her in one-on-one meetings during those months. Her unhappy attitude was casting a pall on the team and creating a lot of counterproductive tension. "I've decided to search for a new provost," I told her. "After more than a year, I just don't think you are a good fit for my leadership team."

I sensed that she was disappointed but not surprised. We agreed that she would move to a position of leading one of our academic departments in her discipline. It turned out to be a good move for her and the university, for she provided a real spark for the department and it thrived under her leadership until she moved on to be provost at a university in another state.

A New Provost

As we always did in the public universities where I served, we initiated the search for a new provost by establishing a search committee to solicit applications and nominations, and evaluate them to identify the best candidates for filling our needs. We did this in May, 2008, with a beginning target date of July 1 for the new provost. I realized that this timeline was aggressive and accepted that I may have to revise the start date. In my charge to the search committee, I emphasized the characteristics desired in the successful candidate. "He or she must set the tone for the division of academic affairs, be able to operate as 'first among equals,' and lead by example and persuasion rather than fiat." I further stated that he/she must also be:

- qualified for appointment as a professor with tenure;
- a seasoned and successful academic administrator/leader;
- one who values collegiality and teamwork;
- a self-starter who works hard and strives for perfection;
- a person with excellent oral and written communication skills;
- a person of great integrity;
- one who can move my agenda; and
- a person who has the potential to be a president.

"Finally I ask that, as the object of your work, you recommend to me three to five well-qualified, unranked candidates to invite for interviews. Please remember that you are a search committee, not a selection committee. I will make the final hiring decision."

Of the three candidates the search committee recommended, only one seemed to possess the combination of experience, skills, and mindset to satisfy my requirements. This candidate had experience as a department chair and a provost for a short time. His responses to my interview questions did not excite me, but suggested that his values, work ethic, and vision were consistent with my own and, therefore, might lead to a successful working relationship. This and the fact that he seemed to understand what it means to be a team player led me to hire Dr. Richard Jamison as the next provost for Bowie State University. He began work at the university on September 1, 2008.

With any new direct report, I always made it a point to state clearly my expectations for performance standards, and met with the new provost soon after the appointment was announced. "I'm delighted to have you as a member of my leadership team and really believe that our work together will move the university to new heights!" I said. "I want to be as clear as possible in describing my expectations for you, since how well you meet them will be the basis of my annual evaluation of your performance."

"Good," he said. "That should be very helpful."

"First, I want you to promote my goals, objectives, values, and agenda. I want you to be efficient and timely in handling assignments, and to give me timely and conscientious advice on matters affecting the university. Second, I need you to be an effective communicator. Ask questions when you need clarification. Respond to my telephone calls, emails, and text messages. Third, be a sound decision-maker and do not confront me with any surprises. Fourth, always bring at least one feasible solution to every problem or challenge. And fifth, I want you to be first among equals; be a great team player; be quick to take a university perspective rather than a more limited divisional one; and be a leader among the team members. Do you have any questions about any of that?"

"No, it's very clear and I have no problems with any of it."

"Great! We're starting this relationship on the same page!"

By December, I started to feel that it was time for the new provost to be making a larger contribution to the leadership of the university than I was seeing. "Richard," I told him, "I really need you to step up and help us meet the goals that I set for the university for this year."

"Well, I've been working pretty hard to make my office comfortable and conducive to work for me. I've gotten some curtains up and just need to replace some carpeting, and have some painting done so I can really be productive," he shared. I was starting to get the picture of how important his comfort was, as I remembered seeing him walk around the provost's office suite in his bare socks. From my perspective, some idiosyncrasies are tolerable as long as the work gets done on time. Besides, I knew that he was an "arts" person when we hired him, so I was prepared for some variation in style and approach.

"I understand, and certainly want you to feel comfortable in your work environment. But I really need you to start focusing on the objectives that we agreed on for this year."

"All right. I'll work on them with more urgency. I almost have the office the way I want it now."

"Good," I said, thinking he only needed a gentle nudge to get him moving in the right direction.

I expected some noticeable change in his behavior over the next few weeks but, to my dismay, only saw the earlier pattern continued. In April, I began my usual process of annual evaluation for my direct reports. Looking specifically at the provost's accomplishments toward meeting his objectives, I became disappointed to the point of alarm. His failure to meet his objectives meant that some of my own objectives would be unmet for the year and negatively affect Kirwan's evaluation of my performance! I tried to put the best spin I could on my own annual report with phrases like, "This assessment activity was postponed because of the organizational and staffing changes that the provost had to make upon arriving at BSU," and "This metric was dropped for FY09 to give the new provost more time to set up and become acclimated to Bowie State University." I did not like being put in this situation and I was determined to prevent its happening again!

To be as clear as possible, I followed-up my year-end evaluation meeting with this provost with a letter reiterating my critical points: "As I related at that time, . . . your overall performance . . . was less than satisfactory." " . . . my principal disappointment with your performance derives from the fact that you did not embrace, pursue, or achieve some of the key presidential objectives which had been assigned to the provost for the year."

> "Though the tone of this letter is, of necessity, critical, I note that overall you did contribute to the advancement of BSU's mission during 2008-09 and the institution is better because of that. As I said during our session last week, you have all of the ingredients—intellect, experience, and instinct—to be an outstanding provost. You must, however, focus your energies and talents on the critical objectives for the institution and pursue them with passion and a commitment to excellence and success. It is imperative that I see this change between now and December 31, 2009."

I could see by the middle of November that Jamison would not make the progress that I had hoped for and insisted upon. For the good of the university, I needed to make a change in this position, and I had learned that once it's clear that a change needs to be made, the best policy is to do it quickly. Hence, I now had to face the task of removing him and beginning another search process for this vital university position. Though, for me, removing an employee from a job is never easy, I was able to move forward in good conscience because I had communicated with him where he was falling short, what I needed him to accomplish and by when, and the consequences of failure. He should not be surprised that I was taking this action.

I sent him a reassignment letter that opened with: "Please be advised that, according to our earlier discussion, effective January 1, 2010, through June 30, 2010, you will serve as Special Assistant to the President" His salary and benefits would remain intact throughout that transition period as we searched for his successor, and he was to work on the specific objectives delineated in the letter.

By all counts, this transition represented a failure. I had replaced one poor fit for provost with another, and now found myself beginning another search—all in fifteen months! It didn't look good but, more importantly, my failure to fill this position with the right person was hindering the progress of the university. Bowie State University deserved better, and I was determined to get it right!

The Second New Provost

I charged the search committee with beginning the second provost search in earnest in March 2010. We sought the same attributes for the right candidate as we did in the first search; we just had to do a much better job of finding the person possessing them! By May, the committee had recommended three finalists for campus interviews and they were scheduled for later that month. The fact that two of them were women was an unexpected bonus, since it meant there was a good chance that our next provost would add to my leadership team's gender diversity. Given that more than 60 percent of our enrollment was women, I thought it especially desirable to have women in top leadership positions.

Again, on paper, all three finalists seemed well-qualified for the position. One of them, though, stood out from the rest. Dr. Terri Stanton had worked at an HBCU similar to Bowie State, had been very successful in grant writing and fundraising, and she held a PhD in computer science from a top-tier university! *Wow!* I thought. *How special would that be—to have our new provost be the holder of a prestigious doctorate in a STEM discipline*! The STEM disciplines—science, technology, engineering, and mathematics—are very hot at all educational levels these days, and this would be a real plus for BSU! During my one-on-one interview with her in my sitting room, I occupied my usual seat in the armchair facing the door to the outer office and she sat on the couch to my left beneath my Romare Bearden serigraph, "School Bell Time."

"Dr. Stanton," I asked, "why do you think you can succeed in this job when others have had such difficulty?"

With an ever-so-slight smile, she glanced down toward the coffee table in front of her and answered: "I grasp things quickly, and because I don't need much sleep, I tend to work on projects for many hours straight through. Therefore, I can get a lot done in short order."

She had shared this with an air that suggested a high level of self-confidence. I was impressed with both the response and the confidence! In addition, around the time of the interview, one of my University System of Maryland presidential colleagues had pulled me aside at a system-wide meeting.

"Mickey, one of my proteges has applied for your provost position. She has good experience and credentials and I think she'd be a good provost for Bowie." I viewed his endorsement of Stanton as confirmation that she was the person to hire!

To my great delight, Stanton accepted our offer and began work at BSU in the fall of 2010. I felt that I had finally gotten the provost position right and we would soon start reaping the benefits. Stanton's first month or so went just as I had expected, based on what I had learned during the interview process. She tackled assignments forthrightly and completed them in short order. She prioritized those things that were highest on my list of objectives and didn't seem to be deterred by resistance to change or the slower pace that some faculty and staff on campus preferred.

Alright, I thought. *Provost Stanton is off to a great start!*

Friday, September 24, began like any other Friday standing between me and a weekend. I arrived at the office at my usual time, around 8:30 a.m., and started to plan my day by examining my calendar. That's when a scheduled meeting caught my eye and set off alarm bells in my head. The meeting was with a group of five or six faculty members. James Jones, the self-proclaimed, longtime nemesis of BSU presidents, was listed first among the participants. Dr. Ann Nedd, chair of the English Department, was the other name that I recognized immediately. *What is this about?* I wondered. Instinctively, I knew they were coming to talk to me about something that displeased them, but had no clue as to what it was.

When they arrived for the meeting, the office receptionist greeted them and ushered them into the conference room right off the reception area, the same one we used for our weekly cabinet meetings. The faculty group took seats at the circular conference table directly opposite the door to my office so that I faced them immediately upon entering the conference room.

"Good morning!" I said. "What can I do for you this morning?"

Jones spoke up, revealing that he was the spokesperson for the group. I wondered if he was leading the group, or if he had been recruited to be their spokesperson. "We came to let you know that we can't work with her!"

"You can't work with whom?" I asked. "What are you talking about?"

"Dr. Stanton. We can't work with her," he repeated as he shook his head from side to side to emphasize his point.

I found it interesting to note that this group purporting to represent "the faculty" was not comprised of officers or elected members of the Faculty Senate, the official representative body of the faculty, but decided to not challenge them on it at that time. "What happened?" I asked. "Why can't you work with her?"

"She doesn't know how to talk to people," Jones said. "She made changes to the curriculum without faculty participation, she made some personnel changes without giving people proper notice, and we're not going to work with her!"

"Ok, I hear what you're saying," I said. "This is the first I've heard of this and I must admit, I'm very surprised. I thought she was off to a great start, so I'll need a few days to gather the facts and decide what action, if any, needs to be taken." In the moment, I remembered the initial warning that Kirwan had given me about Jones, as well as my meeting with him when he told me that he had personally led votes of "no confidence" against the university's last three presidents.

"We can't work with her. You know what you have to do," Jones declared.

"Again, I hear you clearly. But I will have to gather the facts and make my own determination. And even if I confirm that she has been violating our core values, I would want to treat her as I would want to be treated. I'd want to give her a chance to show that she can make the necessary changes."

"You do what you have to do or we'll take action against you and her!" Jones said. The others sitting around the table demonstrated their agreement by their silence. I recognized this as a threat to make me the fourth consecutive BSU president to experience a "no confidence" vote, and that prospect was disturbing!

At this point, Nedd spoke up: "President Burnim, we don't have anything against you. We think you're doing a good job, but Dr. Stanton is another matter."

I thanked them for bringing this matter to my attention and reiterated that I wanted all campus employees to treat others with dignity and respect at all times. "I'll look into this right away."

As promised, I immediately launched my personal investigation of the Stanton's interaction with BSU's faculty and staff to see if there really was something to the charges made by my faculty visitors. Over the next several days, I talked to several faculty and staff members across the campus whom I trusted, and asked about their experiences with Provost Stanton. I also consulted with several prominent leaders in the faculty and staff senates. The messages that I received back were clear! I heard, for example, that "Dr. Stanton talks down to people, sometimes belittles them, and sometimes moves ahead independently on matters that should be addressed through a shared governance approach." Also, "She does not adhere to our core values and has already created a lot of ill-will across the campus."

So there was some substance to the charges of the faculty delegation! While taking in this reality, I sat at my desk and gazed out of my office window, not really focusing on anything, but deep in thought. "Lord, what's the best way for me to address this situation?" I asked. I was inclined to give Stanton a chance to adjust her behavior and make amends with the faculty and staff. *She's very bright, she has the energy and work ethic to do the job, and she still has the potential to be a great asset for BSU, I mused. On the other hand, I have no doubt that Jones and his supporters will orchestrate a vote of "no confidence" in my leadership if I don't remove her.* At that point, a Bible verse came to mind: "May integrity and uprightness protect me, because my hope is in you." (Psalm 25:21) It was now clearer. My job is to try to do what is right while being truthful and honest. I picked up the telephone receiver and pushed the intercom button for my executive assistant. "Mrs. Ward: please call the provost's office and make an appointment for Dr. Stanton to come over so we can discuss an important matter."

When Stanton arrived, Ward buzzed to inform me. "Show her into the sitting room," I said.

I walked through my office door to the sitting room just as Stanton was entering through the door from Ward's area. I sat in my usual chair, the upholstered armchair with its back to the window, facing the door to Ward's area. Stanton sat on the couch.

"Dr. Stanton, a few days ago I was visited by a faculty delegation led by Dr. James Jones. They had come to complain about you and to let me know that they could not work with you!" As I recall, Stanton showed no visible reaction to my report, but revealed her signature slight smile and declared, "I have been moving pretty fast, but I can straighten this out."

"Good. Please do that as quickly as you can!"

Mid-morning on Friday, October 8, Ward walked into my office and I immediately noticed something in her hand. "President Burnim, this letter was just hand-delivered to the office." The letter was signed by several faculty members, including the ones who had met with me a few days earlier, but did not include signatures from the Faculty Senate's leadership. The letter committed to writing the charges that were made to me in person earlier, with references to shared governance and leadership styles, and requested a meeting with Provost Stanton and myself at a specific location on October 14.

This small group of faculty members is trying to usurp the authority of the Faculty Senate, I thought. Not only was the letter not from the senate, but Provost Stanton and the Executive Committee of the Faculty Senate had already scheduled a Faculty Association meeting for October 21, where such issues and concerns could be discussed. In fact, Senate President Olusola Akinyele had already sent out an announcement about the meeting to the entire faculty.

The issues of shared governance and observation of our core values of civility and respect are important and I intended to resolve the breakdowns that had been pointed out. *Should I respond to this letter?* I wondered. *If this group is trying to undermine or circumvent the official Faculty Senate, then my responding could serve to give them legitimacy. If I don't respond, this group will likely charge that I don't listen and am unresponsive to faculty concerns. Furthermore, this is an attempt to strong-arm me. I've already met with them, heard their concerns, and told them I would investigate and take appropriate action.*

After mulling it over, I chose to not respond to the letter. Instead, I wrote an open letter to the entire faculty reminding them of the meeting the provost and the Executive Committee of the Senate had scheduled, and encouraging them to attend and express their concerns.

As soon as I came into the office on October 22, my chief of staff, Tammi Thomas, rushed in from her office to meet me. "President Burnim," she said, "this morning's

Washington Post blog includes a headline that you need to see." The printout in her hand was titled, "A No-confidence Vote in Bowie State's Leadership."

"Oh, my goodness! What happened?"

"Apparently, Dr. Jones presided over the Faculty Association meeting last night, and led votes of "No Confidence" in Provost Stanton and you."

"But Dr. Jones is no longer the Faculty Senate chair," I protested. "Dr. Akinyele is the chair now!"

"Well, he was, but somehow Dr. Akinyele was removed from office last weekend while he was at a math conference on the west coast and replaced by Dr. Jones."

"What? That's crazy!"

"I know; but it seems that's what happened. According to this blog, the vote was 68 to 2 for 'No Confidence' in Dr. Stanton, and 49 to 8 for 'No Confidence' in you."

There were 229 full-time faculty members at the university that fall, all of whom would have been eligible to participate in the Faculty Association meeting, so this action was taken under the direction of possibly illegitimate leadership with likely less than a third of the faculty participating.

Suddenly I feel wounded. I'd been giving my all to this university for four years and, by the grace of God, it had made a lot of progress under my leadership! Our enrollment was up; fundraising had improved; and we enjoyed a growing positive reputation in the Maryland general assembly and among members of the Board of Regents! Furthermore, I'd gone to great lengths to lead in an open and inclusive way. The faculty members who met with me readily admitted that they had no problem with me, but really wanted to get rid of Stanton. How unfair, then, was it to sully my reputation with this vote to try to force me to fire the provost!

I was not entirely surprised to be in a situation like this, given the warning that Kirwan had given me during our initial meeting at the airport and Jones' proud announcement that he personally had led votes of no confidence against the three presidents that immediately preceded me. How would I deal with this? What would be best for the university?

Being mindful of the "No Surprises" rule, I called my boss, Kirwan. "Brit," I said, "this morning's *Washington Post* reported that the Bowie State faculty took 'No Confidence' votes in both Provost Jones and me at a meeting last night."

"What happened?"

"I'm not sure since I wasn't given the courtesy of direct notification, but it appears that the Faculty Senate chair, Dr. Akinyele, was removed from office while he was away from campus and was replaced by James Jones, who presided over last night's meeting." I then recounted my meeting with the faculty group a couple of weeks earlier and the threat that Jones had made.

"Well, thanks for letting me know and keep me informed as it unfolds."

"Okay, I certainly will."

When I got home at the end of that day and walked through the door leading from the garage to the kitchen, I called out, "Hey Dear! I'm home." LaVera came from the den to meet me and we embraced with a brief kiss as we usually did. Then, as she held me at arms-length, her facial expression changed from one of warm greeting to concern. She looked into my eyes and asked, "What's wrong?"

After forty-one years of marriage, I couldn't keep anything from her even if I wanted to. I led her to the couch and told her what had happened. Her usually smiling face revealed a combination of concern and anger.

"Babe, I'm sorry. You've been doing a great job and don't deserve this kind of attack," she said as we embraced each other. She was always supportive and always loving! As we ended the embrace, she asked, "What are you going to do?"

"I'm not sure yet, but I'll pray and seek God's guidance."

The next day, I decided it was time to have another conversation with Stanton about this situation and directed Ward to ask her to come to my office.

"Terri, you told me that you could fix this rift with the faculty," I said to Stanton when she arrived. "Have you met with them yet?"

"No, I haven't yet."

"Well, these "No Confidence" votes, though taken by a small percentage of the faculty, have escalated things."

"I'll speak to them."

"Good. Do it soon."

When I checked in with Kirwan a couple of days later, he shared with me something that one of the board members had said to him. I was taken aback when he quoted a powerful and influential member of the board as having said, "I hope Mickey can survive this!"

Why wouldn't I survive it? I had handled the situation in a very reasonable manner thus far. I had listened to the complaint, investigated to confirm its validity, and was working with Stanton to take corrective action. From my perspective, the vote of "No Confidence" in my leadership was completely unjustified and was probably in violation of the Faculty Senate's own constitution and by-laws. I would survive if the board supported me, and I thought they had good reason to do so!

As a Christian, however, I relied on Jesus Christ for guidance and protection. I had followed what I believed to be good tenets of leadership—be a good listener, ascertain the facts, take appropriate action expeditiously, and treat people as I would want to be treated—and yet my presidency was being seriously threatened!

So what? I had to live with myself and that meant doing the right thing. I knew that God would answer my prayers for direction and guidance in dealing with this crisis, so I decided to continue following those leadership principles and deal with whatever consequences arose.

I wanted to be patient in choosing the proper next step in moving this crisis to some resolution, as I really hoped that Provost Stanton would be able to right her relationship with the faculty. I knew, however, that the longer this situation festered without resolution, the more likely that Jones, with his enablers and supporters, would try to escalate things further. Also, though the board of regents had promised to be very supportive if the relationship with this group came to a head, I wanted to resolve this without it reaching that point. The majority of the faculty needed to see that I was sensitive to their concerns and taking reasonable steps to make things better. Stanton's conversation with faculty leaders was the key.

"Mrs. Ward," I said, "please call Dr. Stanton and ask her to come over."

When Stanton arrived, I rose and gestured for her to take a seat at the small round table in my office. This situation called for greater intensity than the more relaxed setting of my sitting room would suggest.

"Terri, have you met with the faculty leaders yet?" I asked.

"Not yet. I've been really busy working on some other things that I need to finish."

"Terri, we're in a tight spot here and I need to show some movement to resolve it."

"Well, go ahead and do whatever you need to do."

Her response surprised me. I wondered if she had considered what my action might be. I decided that she had thought about it and her response indicated she was resigned to losing her job if it came to that.

"In that case, I think we are at a point where you go or we both go. So I'm letting you go effective immediately. I've talked to Brit and he has agreed to give you an assignment at the UM Systems office for the remainder of this academic year at your current salary. I know that you worked hard and were making some progress and I appreciate it. And I'm sorry that things have reached this point."

"What will be the assignment?" she asked.

"I don't know, but you'll find out when you get there. You should report there tomorrow morning."

I called a town hall meeting with the faculty for the next day. There was no need to announce the meeting topic. Everyone on campus knew what was brewing. The meeting was held in the gymnasium and, as would be expected, it was well attended. Since it was Veterans Day, I began the meeting by paying tribute and appreciation to our veterans. Then I shared my prepared remarks:

> We have been through what I would describe as a traumatizing period. A number of things have been done and said that have evoked very strong emotions. A number of people have felt a lot of pain. This experience has affected faculty, staff, and students, so we are holding this town hall meeting in an attempt for us to begin a healing process to enable the university to move beyond this difficult period and to re-focus on the very critical initiatives and efforts before us—things like our Middle States re-affirmation, closing the achievement gap, re-designing courses, etc.
>
> What has happened?
>
> On Tuesday, I met with the provost, Dr. Stanton, and told her that our attempts to move beyond the allegations

and negative feelings that engulfed the campus in the last few weeks had failed and that I had concluded, for the good of the university, to end her service as provost.

I am in the process of naming an interim provost, and do not intend to rush into another search. We need a period of stability and maybe this interim can help.

What can we learn from the experience?

Communications are always critical and can easily fail. From my perspective, much of this turmoil has resulted from failed communications. Words chosen or ill-chosen, words spoken which should have been written, tone, context, body language, volume, inflection, the attitude of the listener or reader—all of these elements are critical when effective communication is at stake. It involves making sure that what was said is the same thing that was heard.

Our core values, particularly civility and integrity, are vitally important for us to honor at all times. This includes what we say to others, how we say it, and whether we do what we say.

We have the capacity to solve campus problems and issues internally. In my administration, we have worked hard to be open and transparent. I prefer and encourage people to follow the established channels of communication when seeking resolution, but I don't believe that anyone who has persisted in trying to get an appointment with me has ultimately been denied. My point is that if there's an important issue that needs addressing, bring it to my attention and I will do so. Let me hasten to add, though, that doesn't mean that I will do exactly what you are requesting, or within the time frame that you would like.

I try to be a careful and deliberate person, and one who lives by the Golden Rule. I try to determine what are the facts, not just what are the thoughts, feelings, and perceptions. That often involves talking to different people, requesting and reviewing documents, and being very careful to draw my own conclusions based on the facts ascertained.

How do we move forward?

- Recognize and acknowledge that the university and its mission should take priority when it comes to decisions regarding people and activities on the campus.
- Address important matters to the appropriate people in a responsible and professional manner. Use our shared governance vehicles and give those units a reasonable chance to act.
- Honor our core values—excellence, civility, integrity, diversity, and accountability.
- Work really hard at being effective communicators. Realize that what was said might not be exactly the same as what was heard. Give people the benefit of the doubt.

We also need to have some conversations about the meaning and interpretation of "shared governance."

I will now open up the floor for questions and comments. As I do so, however, I ask you to remember and practice our core value of civility. If we disagree, let's do so without being disagreeable.

From that point, the meeting went smoothly. Since the provost was leaving, there was nothing more to fight about . . .

for the moment. Karen Johnson Shaheed, our general counsel who had previously served as secretary of the Maryland Higher Education Commission, accepted my assignment as interim provost and performed that role from November, 2010, until July 1, 2012. She provided steady, calming leadership for the Academic Affairs Division as we healed from the turmoil we had experienced. In addition to continuing to work on the aforementioned priorities, we faced the added challenge of a struggling state economy, which required planning and preparing for significant cuts to our operating budget.

THE THIRD NEW PROVOST

The Terri Stanton experience traumatized both the university and me. Rather than rush right into another search, I thought the university needed some time to heal. I also needed to do some serious reflection about these two failed attempts to hire persons who had both had the requisite skills and the temperament to do the job. Hence, I asked Karen Shaheed to commit to serving as interim provost for at least a year. *That should give us enough time to figure out what had gone wrong and how to give ourselves the best chance of getting it right the next time*, I thought.

Interim Vice President Shaheed brought the same level of stability to the position that she did when I called on her the first time. Decisions were made on time, communications were crisp, and the routine work of the office was done smoothly and efficiently. A little over a year later, we had enjoyed a period of calm that allowed us to get through two commencements and a budget/legislative season, and I felt that the time was right to begin another search for a permanent provost.

I was tempted to just appoint Shaheed to the permanent position, but knew that because we were a public state-assisted university, we were obligated to go through a formal open process. Hence, we would have to advertise for the position, and accept and screen applications. The process would have to avoid any kind of favoritism or illegal discrimination. I was also strongly committed to having an experienced traditional academic in the role—one who had come up through the faculty ranks and could bring a faculty perspective to the leadership of the Academic Affairs Division of the university.

Having hired two provosts who both failed to succeed in the position at Bowie State led some to doubt my judgment. A member of the board of regents was heard musing out loud, "This causes me to question Mickey's judgment." And though my boss, system Chancellor Brit Kirwan, was very supportive throughout the ordeal, I suspected that he, too, was feeling some pressure from the board to make this provost problem at Bowie State go away. I knew, however, that his primary concern was for the welfare of the entire university system and this included the stability and effectiveness of each of the constituent institutions within it. I felt that I had to get it right this time.

What's the best way to proceed this time? What were the major factors in the two failed searches? What do I need to do differently this time? These were the questions floating through my head as we moved to begin this third search for the right provost. In developing solutions and strategies, I always try to carefully analyze the relevant facts, and consult with persons who have expertise and good judgment. Then I pray for wisdom and guidance in moving forward.

What did I do wrong in the first search?

I didn't give enough weight to an obvious warning sign. The first provost had previously served as provost at another university for a very short period of time. He asserted that the short tenure owed to the arrival of a new president who wanted to hire his own person. I thought this was a very plausible explanation and elected to hire him on the basis of his otherwise excellent experience. My failure came from not fully investigating the possibility that his tenure was so short because the new president was able to see very quickly that the provost he inherited was not going to work out! Okay, I would intensify my guard against making similar erroneous assumptions during this third search!

What about the second search? What led to my failure that time?

That candidate seemed to check all of the requisite boxes—good academic track record, STEM discipline, significant experience at a university similar to BSU, and the personal endorsement of a highly respected colleague. *So what happened?* Some months after the second provost's ninety-day tenure became public, I ran into the president of the university where she had worked prior to her arrival at BSU. We had known each other as colleagues for many years.

"Mickey," he said, "if you had called me, I could have told you about the danger of hiring this person."

Then it hit me. During the interview, Stanton had asked me not to contact the president since she would likely suffer repercussions if she didn't get the job. I chose to honor her request and talk to other persons with whom she worked at that university, but did not call the president. This was the mistake that led to the second wrong provost choice! I vowed to never again violate my own protocol of talking directly to the immediate direct supervisor of persons I was considering for a key position.

The third search went smoothly and the search committee sent me a list of three candidates they considered highly qualified for the job. I quickly identified Dr. Weldon Jackson, a political scientist, who had risen through the academic ranks to become a tenured professor and who had also served as provost at his alma mater, Morehouse College. The president under whom Jackson had served as provost was no longer at Morehouse, but I tracked him down in another state in an attempt to gain any insight that he could provide about Jackson's service as provost in his administration.

"Dr. Jackson is a good man and he works hard," he said. "He faced some special circumstances when he worked with me at Morehouse, but he handled them well. I recommend that you give him a chance."

I believed that this president was a man of integrity and I trusted him. Hence, the report from the search committee and the references, whom I talked to directly, all led me to conclude that Jackson was the right choice. He began work as Bowie State's provost on July 1, 2012.

About the job he was doing, I wrote in my journal almost a year later:

"Praise God! I give thanks to God for directing my decision regarding who to hire as provost a year ago. Weldon Jackson is a man of God who has tremendous experience and wisdom. He is doing a superb job!"

He led the Academic Affairs Division until I retired in 2017. My prayer had indeed been answered!

Leading the CIAA

Sometimes the opportunity to serve comes as a result of an unexpected organizational need. A position vacancy suddenly occurs because its occupant received a better offer, or because of a serious illness, or death. And then sometimes the economic or political circumstances call for a different kind of leadership and the organization's fiduciary stewards move to install the leadership that's needed at that time. Effective leadership guides an organization through difficult times so that focus of its core mission is maintained and progress continues. At one point, my university's athletics association provided me with just such a challenge.

I spent most of my time every day at my desk in the inner office of the president's suite. It was a large rectangular one with a hardwood veneer and it faced the door to my sitting room. When that door was open, as it was this quiet Monday morning in May, I could enjoy the view of my Bearden serigraph mounted on the far wall. That's exactly what I was doing when, at about ten o'clock, the intercom buzzer startled me.

"President Burnim," Dr. Suber from Saint Augustine's College is calling for you," my executive assistant informed me.

"Hey, Diane," I greeted her as I picked up the phone. "What's happening?"

Diane Suber and I had been friends for a number of years. We became colleagues in North Carolina when she was named president of St. Augustine College in Raleigh and I was serving as chancellor of ECSU. Our paths crossed often at state-level higher education meetings, at regional meetings like the annual conference of the Southern Association of Colleges and Schools, and at national gatherings like the annual meeting of the National Association for Equal Opportunity in Higher Education. It was our common affiliation with the Central Intercollegiate Athletic Association (CIAA), however, that gave us the greatest opportunity to get to know each other. For many years the CIAA had been widely recognized as the premier collegiate athletic conference among HBCUs. We were twelve colleges and universities strong and provided competitive opportunities for our student athletes in ten or so sports, with basketball being the most recognizable, respected, and enduring. Suber and I, along with the presidents and chancellors of the other member institutions, comprised the board of directors for the conference, and it was through our many athletic conference-related activities that we really came to know each other. One of the board's primary responsibilities was to provide support and oversight to the conference commissioner, who was the administrator and day-to-day leader for conference operations.

"Hey, Mickey," she said. "Are you going to make the meeting on Thursday?"

The meeting to which she referred was our annual CIAA board meeting.

"Yes, I'm planning to go."

"Good! You know this is our May meeting and we will need to elect officers for the next two years."

"Yes, that's right."

"Dot and I were talking and we agreed that the next two or three years will be critical for our conference and we will need a sure, steady hand to guide us through this period."

"Yes, it certainly will be critical," I agreed. "The conference fund reserve needs to be increased so we will be better prepared for down years and revenue streams need to be diversified so we are not so dependent on the basketball tournament receipts."

"Also, the public relations nightmare that the city of Charlotte is going through because of its convention manager's alleged mishandling of funds could have some blow back for the CIAA because of his work with our commissioner," Diane added. "There are also our conference expansion challenges to negotiate. We certainly will need a steady hand to guide the board through the next couple of years and Dot and I agreed that you would be the right person to do it!"

"Wait! What are you talking about?" I protested. "I just finished my term as board chair a couple of years ago." Board officers were elected for two-year terms and I had served as chair just a few years earlier.

"We know, but your leadership style is more likely to be able to hold us together and help us to move forward in harmony. Your calm, reasoned approach is less likely to create personality conflicts, and the guys on the board are more likely to listen to you than one of us," she suggested.

I leaned back in my leather executive chair to consider what my colleague had just said. As I thought about it, I agreed that she and Dot were probably correct in their assessment. Then my chest stuck out a little further and my head started to swell . . . but this was only a brief concession to my ego.

They were both genuinely concerned about the future of the conference and thought this was the best way forward. Both of them are gifted leaders but they believed the other board members would be more inclined to listen to me and follow my lead, both because of personality differences and maybe a tinge of sexism that so permeates our society. In spite of that I still was not anxious to be chair again so soon after my last term. Besides, the current board secretary was probably expecting to be elected chair. This was not mandated by the conference by-laws, but it was traditional. Hence, my entering into the chairmanship election process had the potential of creating tension and ill-feeling. "Ok, Diane," I finally responded. "If I am nominated, I will stand for election."

On the morning of the second day of the board meeting, we reached the "Election of Officers" agenda item and the board chair called on the board secretary, who was also chair of the nominations committee, for the committee report. "I don't have a report," he admitted, "but we can get one together pretty quickly."

"Let's just open the floor for nominations for each office and vote on those nominated," Diane suggested. Out of the corner of my eye, I perceived a slight flinch by the secretary, as if he wanted to raise an objection as he realized that any control he might have had over the election process was slipping away.

The board chair, appearing unsure of how to proceed, turned to the commissioner's staff person, who usually provided guidance on matters of parliamentary procedure, and who proffered, "You can do that as long as it's permitted by the by-laws and that's the will of the board."

At that point, President Suber said in her usual very deliberate and articulate manner, "Mr. Chairman, I nominate Mickey Burnim to serve as chair of the board of directors."

"I second the motion," chimed in President Yancey. "Are there other nominations?" asked the chair. As I recall, the board secretary was also nominated. With no additional nominations, the chair called for the vote, and I was elected by a slim margin.

I smiled outwardly while sighing inwardly. The smile was a show of appreciation for the board members who had expressed their confidence in me by voting for me, and the sigh was acknowledgment to myself that I would have preferred not serving another term as board chair at that point.

The next couple of years for our athletic conference turned out to be exactly what presidents Suber and Yancey had predicted. The city of Charlotte, North Carolina, which hosted the conference's annual basketball tournament, went through some turmoil in 2011 and the CIAA Board saw this as a threat to the tournament. This was especially troublesome because the tournament was the single-largest revenue source for the annual operation of the conference. The Charlotte City Council had issues with the Charlotte Regional Visitors Authority (CRVA), which was headed by an executive director who had been a critical conduit for the CIAA in conducting the tournament and other conference operations in Charlotte. The CRVA board hired the consulting firm of PricewaterhouseCoopers to do an assessment of the CRVA. According to one source, the resulting report "cited a need for revamped internal policies for bonuses and entertainment expenses . . ."⁹ Because of allegations like those reported by WCNC News, which referred to CRVA's "lavish spending . . . to lure events to Charlotte," the other board members and I became concerned about the possibility of the CIAA being dragged into this controversy since we were one of the events "lured" to Charlotte. All of this turmoil surrounding the CRVA led the CIAA Board to decide, as a proactive measure, to have its own assessment done, and we hired a local firm to conduct a forensic audit.

As this situation was unfolding, the CIAA Commissioner announced his decision to retire after twenty-two years and the board was faced with having to find new leadership for the conference in addition to following up on any recommendations that might come from its assessment report. The timing of his departure, November 14, 2011, just three months before the conference basketball tournament, further complicated the transition.

The fall of 2011 was turning out to be a very turbulent time for the conference, one fraught with multiple land mines, any one of which could spell disaster for the CIAA. My mind churned with the uncertainties. *How were we going to pull off a successful tournament in just three months without the person who had coordinated it for the last twenty-two years? How were we going to manage media and public relations so that tournament ticket sales would not be adversely affected during this period? What would we do in the event of a weather catastrophe that necessitated our canceling the tournament? What would happen to the conference if it were somehow sucked into the emerging vortex of CRVA politics? How would we find the right person to lead the conference to follow a long-term commissioner who had led it from relative obscurity to national prominence?*

Wow! Why did I agree to take on this chairmanship again knowing that it had the potential for adding these weighty matters to my personal portfolio in addition to my job of leading Bowie

State University, for which I was being paid? Too late now! I was in it and I needed to give it my best!

As board chair, it fell to me to be the conference's spokesperson in the wake of the commissioner's sudden retirement. Hence, I agreed to make a statement and answer questions during a telephone press conference on the afternoon of November 15. Sitting at my desk, I made notes in preparation for the call. I had learned during my time as provost at NCCU that dealing with the press could be tricky. I needed to be truthful in answering questions, but careful to not put the CIAA at risk by saying something revealing legally confidential information, things that were easily subject to misinterpretation, or things that could be unnecessarily embarrassing to other people.

What questions was I sure to be asked and what were the best responses to those questions? Also, what messages did I want to give no matter what questions were asked? I rehearsed the following questions and answers.

> Q: "Why did the commissioner decide to retire just three months before the tournament?"
> A: "I could speculate, but the commissioner himself is the best person to speak to the timing of his decision and announcement."
> Q: "Was he forced out by the board?"
> A: "As I said in my statement, he indicated that, for personal reasons, he decided to retire immediately."
> Q: "Will you name an interim commissioner?"
> A: "Yes. The commissioner's long-time associate commissioner, Monique Smith, has stepped in as interim commissioner."
> Q: "Will there be a search for his successor?"

A: "Yes. I anticipate that we will begin a national search as soon after the tournament in February as is practicable."

No matter what, I wanted to convey an image of calm, purposeful movement. People should come away from the press conference believing that the CIAA was stable and the tournament would run smoothly!

At 4:30 p.m., my executive assistant buzzed my desk telephone and told me that the conference call was open. After thanking the participants, I read a brief prepared statement, which was the same one that had been released to the press the day before. I then invited questions from the press.

"Why did Commissioner Kerry resign so close to the tournament?"

"When will you hire a new commissioner?"

"Who will serve in the interim?"

I smiled to myself as I gave my prepared answers to their anticipated questions, and was pleasantly surprised that there was no suspicion or hostility shown in the questions asked. In less than thirty minutes, I had answered their questions and felt that I had succeeded in showing calm, competent leadership.

The weeks following the press conference were consumed by the activities of addressing the many challenges facing the conference. At the top of the list was our preparation for the CIAA tournament, which was just twelve short weeks away. During this period, I called frequent telephone meetings of the board trying to make sure that we were applying our best collective in thinking about solutions to the obstacles we faced. "Who's the best person to lead the operational logistics leading up to the tournament?" we asked ourselves.

"What about Peggy Davis?" I asked. "She is one of the conference's most successful athletic directors, having coached her team to the conference championship and perennially having them in contention, and she has the reputation of being an excellent administrator."

Peggy Davis was the longtime women's basketball coach at Virginia State University (VSU) who had been elevated by their previous president to serve as director of athletics. She oversaw the university's entire athletics operation, including managing the budget, supervising the head coaches for all the sports, and insuring a working compliance function.

"Yes, she would be great," chimed in VSU President Dr. Keith Miller. "And though it would be a sacrifice, we would allow her to serve the conference in this capacity if VSU is reimbursed for her services."

"Of course we'll reimburse you," I assured him.

With President Miller's permission, I called Davis the following week and asked if she would serve as interim commissioner through the tournament and until the board could conduct a search for a permanent commissioner. She readily agreed and offered to drive to Bowie to discuss the terms of her interim service.

A month after the press conference, Davis and I met in my office at Bowie State. She is a tall, striking woman who's probably in her early to mid-fifties, but looks younger. "Thank you, Coach Davis, for taking on this assignment," I said. "The board's primary concern is the well-being of the conference. We want you to run the conference to the best of your ability using sound business practices, always displaying the highest integrity, and making sure that the board chair is not hit with any surprises. We also want you to be very cost conscious and look for reasonable ways to reduce expenditures."

"I understand, and can do that," she said.

My spirit was lifted by her enthusiasm and confidence, but there was so much to be done and just three months to do it all without the person who had orchestrated it for the last twenty-two years! The CIAA basketball tournament is the third-largest behind the Big East and the Atlantic Coast Conference (ACC). It was founded in 1912 and has been continued over the years. The tournament is a week-long series of activities around the men's and women's basketball contests leading to conference championships on Saturday night. By tradition, it has been a big reunion for alumni and fans from around the country, and an all-around panoply of highly competitive and exciting basketball games. It is also something of a fashion show for people who come to the games dressed to impress. The women are known to wear a lot of leather and fur and many of the men dress as if they are going to church or an important business meeting! The tournament was a big deal for the conference and we needed it to attract and entertain large crowds since the revenue that it generated was such a large part of the conference budget.

I started to tick off a mental checklist of things that needed to be completed:

- Complete signing sponsors.
- Finalize the arrangement of security.
- See that all of the officials and volunteers are in place.
- Finalize arrangements for the teams' hotels and the various universities' headquarters.
- Plan the announcements, presentations, and entertainment.
- Finish plans for the opening luncheon for the student athletes, the City of Charlotte Reception, the Hall of Fame Banquet, and the post-tournament concert.

- Finalize the hotel arrangements for the conference presidents and chancellors, and their special guests.

Whew! So much to do and so many things that could go wrong. Davis, however, went on to do an amazing job of orchestrating the final preparations for the tournament, and it was a big success. She saw to it that all of those tasks were attended to with no major snafus.

That year, the Shaw University women's team won their second consecutive tournament in a run that eventually led to four straight! The Winston-Salem State University Rams won the men's tournament that year. Though the BSU teams did not reach the finals, my guests and I really enjoyed the pageantry and competition from the vantage point of my president's box suite high above the court. As always, I liked cheering hard for our teams as they fought to win on the court below, and seeing our cheerleaders in new eye-popping uniforms and our pep band dancing and gyrating to their own music as they tried to encourage our teams to victory! One highlight that I looked forward to each year was when Mr. And Miss Bowie State University and their entourage came by the suite in their business attire and royal shoulder sashes. *That's what it's all about,* I thought, *giving students a chance to have their moment in the spotlight!*

We breathed a big post-tournament sigh of relief and turned our attention to the search process to find a new commissioner. We needed someone who was very good at managing people and budgets, who was a great planner, and who knew both how to bring in sponsors for the conference and how to elevate the experience of our student athletes. Among the finalists who emerged were two men and one woman. One of the men had a solid track record as an athletic administrator. The other one didn't have much high-level experience, and struck me as being one for whom this job would be a big stretch.

The young woman, by contrast, had spent several years at the National Collegiate Athletic Association (NCAA) with some major responsibility for its basketball championships, and she had worked as an administrator in an athletic conference—our own CIAA! I thought, *She looks great on paper. How will she do in the interview?* She was amazing! Standing only about five foot four, her physical appearance was not commanding, but her strong steady voice and responses to our questions showed ample self-confidence and great depth of understanding about intercollegiate athletics and the challenges that many programs were facing nationally. When she said, "I'm a bit nervous and I asked some of my closest friends to pray for me at the exact time of this interview," I was sold. That comment indicated to me that she was a person of integrity, humility, and reverence—three key attributes that I look for when hiring new people. She clearly knew her stuff and would very likely make an outstanding commissioner for the CIAA! When I called for a vote after the interviews, a majority of the board members present quickly and enthusiastically voted for her as our number one choice. Hence, Jacqueline Carpenter (now Jacqie McWilliams) became the first female commissioner for the CIAA and the first African American female conference commissioner in any division of the NCAA! I was happy that we had found a great new commissioner and proud that the CIAA had made history in doing so!

Commissioner McWilliams' first year on the job was also the second year of my second term as chair of the board. I was thankful. Things had gone very well during that first year. All of the conference's sports championships had been executed as expected, the conference's finances had been managed so as to reduce our expenditures and meet conference obligations, we had a successful basketball tournament, mended some relationships with sponsors, avoided some lawsuits, reduced our expenditures, and searched for and hired a new commissioner! I thanked God for guiding me as I tried to lead the conference. I felt humbled and grateful when board members expressed their appreciation for my leadership that year. An excerpt from the November 28, 2012, CIAA Board meeting minutes read:

> Dr. Burnim welcomed the BOD and gave brief comments on the position of the CIAA conference since the arrival of the new Commissioner, Jacqie Carpenter. Members of the BOD congratulated Dr. Burnim and praised his leadership given the transition and challenges that the conference has faced in the past year. The Winston-Salem State (WSSU) football team was recognized for winning the CIAA football championship and for advancing in the NCAA Division II football playoffs. Fayetteville State University's (FSU) volleyball team won the CIAA Championship and advanced to the first round of the NCAA DII Volleyball Championships; St. Augustine's won both the Men's and Women's Cross Country Championships.

To God be the glory for the things He has done!

Because the CIAA basketball tournament was the primary revenue source for financing conference operations, Carpenter's first big public test would be her first tournament. The practices of more than two decades had set the patterns and expectations for the annual tournament, and some changes from the ways of the past were sorely needed. In an early meeting with the new commissioner, I described the challenges threatening the conference. "The conference's cash flow is very weak, so something needs to be done to make sure we can meet our monthly payroll of $50,000 and operational expenses such as hiring officials for our various sports. Also, the associate commissioner who managed our football and basketball operations has left, and those are key sports for the conference. And we're facing some potential legal liability that needs to be managed."

As we sat at the conference table in our first face-to-face board meeting after Carpenter came aboard, all eyes focused on her as I called for the report of the commissioner. She sat to my right at the head of the table. The presidents and chancellors of the conference sat along the sides of the long conference table, and the conference staff sat along the wall on the right side of the room.

"Ladies and Gentlemen," she began, "I am pleased today to give you a ninety-day update and assessment of the conference since I was hired." Carpenter listed the following accomplishments:

- The conference office is fully staffed and we have secured a consultant, at no cost, to assist with our business affairs.
- We have hired a senior associate commissioner to manage football and basketball operations.
- The staff has been charged to seek efficiencies in managing championships and events, travel, and meetings for the conference office and membership, and significantly reduce costs.
- The fall conference championships are taking place as planned and are going smoothly.
- We have begun a rebranding campaign for the conference and have a new logo and tagline we would like for you to approve today.

I felt very proud as our new commissioner gave her report. She was in charge and moving the conference forward as we had hoped! Clearly, the search committee had done a great job and the board's wisdom in hiring her was being revealed!

With Carpenter at the helm, the 2013 basketball tournament, her first, went smoothly. Because of her, I was also able to be more focused on applauding and cheering the BSU men's and women's teams during their contests, and spend more time "friend-raising" in my box suite during the games, greeting and hobnobbing with alumni, friends, and supporters who stopped by. The box suites for the chancellors and presidents were about mid-level of the arena so that half of the 19,000 seats were lower and half were higher. Our suite had twelve cushioned seats with armrests and four stools at a bar behind the cushioned seats facing the basketball court. The suite opened into the arena so that we could enjoy all of the sights and sounds of being in the arena while having more space and flexibility to move around.

This tournament really felt different, and by Thursday of tournament week, that difference was quite palpable. Bowie State had met and defeated Chowan University in the first round. That was good, but Chowan had not won a tournament game since they joined the conference a few years earlier, so that win hardly presaged great tournament success for Bowie. But then the team went on to defeat Lincoln University of Pennsylvania, the number one seed in the North, in the second round! So by Thursday night, BSU had won two games in the tournament and advanced to the semifinal round! Still fresh in my mind were the words of Virginia Union's retired legendary men's coach Dave Robbins when our paths crossed earlier in the week.

"Hello, Coach Robbins!" I said. "How are you doing?"

"I'm doing fine. Thank you. How are you?" I could tell that he wasn't sure who I was, so I told him.

"I'm Mickey Burnim from Bowie State. What do you think of the tournament thus far?"

With that clue, he remembered me.

"I think that Bowie State's squad seems to be playing together well right now, and they are the team to watch as we go deeper into the tournament this week."

Could he be right? Would this be our year? This was my eighteenth year of leading a CIAA university and I had never experienced the thrill of winning a CIAA tournament. Though I was trying to manage my expectations so that I wouldn't be too let down if it didn't happen, my hopeful excitement kept growing!

At about 7 a.m. on Saturday morning of tournament week, the final day of the tournament, I sat at the desk in our suite at the Westin Hotel making final edits to the remarks that I would give at the BSU breakfast in a couple of hours. I smiled to myself and gave thanks for what had been a good tournament week for Bowie State. LaVera and I had started the Saturday morning breakfast tradition seven years earlier during our first tournament after coming to BSU. The breakfast was primarily a gathering for alumni of the university—a way to renew or strengthen their connection to their alma mater. We would dress up in black and gold—our school colors, have a nice breakfast together, and I would tell them about the progress we were making and all of the wonderful things that were happening at the university. We always looked for a way to put students before the gathering to help loosen our donors' purse strings by reminding them why it was important to give to the university.

This year, as we were finishing breakfast, the table chatter in the room was suddenly drowned out by loud band music, which sounded like it was right outside the doors to our breakfast! We looked toward the double doors as someone flung them open and in marched the BSU Pep Band! All twenty-five of them, along with the dancers, marched right into our breakfast room playing some of the same tunes they played during the ball games, and at the same volume! I thought for a moment that our glassware might break from the sound. I had been told that the band would come to the breakfast, but this entrance was over the top! We all smiled after we got over the initial shock. They played for about five minutes and then the drum major blew his whistle three times and all the band members, in unison, went to parade rest.

"Ladies and Gentlemen, the Symphony of Soul Pep Band," I announced as I took the podium. "The band has captured the excitement we all feel as we look forward to tonight's men's championship game!" We were all sky-high with anticipation for the men's finals that night since our Bulldogs would be playing Livingstone College for the championship! After defeating Chowan in the first round, the Bulldogs beat Lincoln University, the number one seed in the North, and Winston-Salem State, the number two seed in the South. And tonight they would face Livingstone, the number one seed in the South and the overall number one seed for the tournament. Bowie State had not won the tournament in ten years. Going all the way back to my days at North Carolina Central University, I had been at CIAA institutions a total of twenty-seven years and had never had the experience of celebrating a CIAA basketball championship. *Might this be the year?*

We gave university highlights, thanked our faithful alumni and supporters, and raised a few thousand dollars at the breakfast, so it was a good morning. And with its adjournment, we were free to check out the cheerleaders exhibition, the Fan Experience, day parties, or any of the other activities. I chose to relax in the hotel and save my energy for some hard cheering during the championship game.

"Babe, let's plan to get to our box suite before the women's game starts," I told LaVera. "That way, we'll be there to be good hosts for alumni and supporters who stop by during the women's game and before our game starts." When their teams are playing, the presidents and first ladies traditionally wear the school colors. I had chosen a black suit with gold pinstripes, a white shirt with black-and-gold cat's eye cuff links, and a gold paisley tie. LaVera wore a black leather pant suit, a gold blouse, and a gold scarf with black polka dots. We felt the approving glances of Bowie State supporters as we walked around the concourse past other box suites headed for the one assigned to Bowie State. We were representing the mighty Bulldog Nation!

"Good evening!" we said, and, "So nice of you to stop by." "How about those Bulldogs?" "I think this might be our year!" "Please help yourself to some food and soft drinks." We tried to be cheerful ambassadors for BSU while basking in the excitement of having our team in the finals.

At nine o'clock, the game announcer's familiar baritone voice demanded attention as he spoke over the public address system: "Ladies and Gentlemen, tonight's CIAA men's championship game features the number one seed Blue Bears of Livingstone College and the Bulldogs of Bowie State University." The pep band was blaring and the cheerleaders were preparing to do their best routines as the teams finished their pre-game warm-up. The Blue Bears had dominated their opponents during the regular season and in the tournament. BSU entered the tournament with a win-loss record of something like 14-13 and a low seed, but we felt we had momentum on our side. Our team was peaking at the right time.

At the opening tip-off, I turned my attention from hosting to watching the game. I try not to show it, but it really irks me when someone tries to strike up a conversation when

I'm trying to enjoy a game. I like to watch the strategies and tactics unfold, and fully appreciate the athleticism and skill displayed by the student athletes; I can't do that and carry on a conversation simultaneously. Livingstone had a size advantage at the center and forward positions, but we managed to trade baskets with them in the early stages of the game so that by halftime, only a few points separated the two teams. It was still anyone's ball game!

After halftime, Head Coach Darryl Brooks' strategy was obvious. Continue to play strong defense, pass the ball around, play as a team, and try to get the ball to Byron Westmoreland. Westmoreland was a six foot four senior forward from Baltimore who had been a solid performer all season, but was really emerging as an all-conference performer during the tournament. The focus on team play and good passes to open players gave Bowie State good shots, which were falling, and Westmoreland's confidence was growing visibly as the game progressed. He was calling for the ball and making spectacular scoring plays when he got it.

As I recall, with five or six minutes left in the game, the Bulldogs led by six or eight points, enough for us to be hopeful, but not enough to assure victory with so much time remaining. The Livingstone players, feeling the pressure, began to take chances—putting up shots more quickly and taking lower percentage shots. The Bulldogs got the rebounds, took the ball down the floor, and fed the ball to Westmoreland. On one play, he received the ball near the three-point line, took a jab step to his left, and drove to his right around his defender toward the basket. Extending the ball in his right hand, like an outstretched eagle's wing, he took a two-step approach and dunked the ball! From that point the Bulldogs extended their lead to double digits and victory was in sight! "Babe," I told LaVera, "I'm going to the floor so I'll be there when the game ends!"

As the final buzzer sounded, the BSU players, cheerleaders, and students rushed to the floor in celebration! I stood on the edge of the court, watching the celebration with a big smile. These young men had done it! They had beaten the odds and brought home the first men's tournament championship in ten years, and I was experiencing this jubilation for the very first time. I was very proud of the team and coaches and very thankful for the joy that we now felt because of the win. Confetti rained from the arena rafters as I walked over to Coach Brooks on the floor.

"Congratulations, Coach! This is sweet!"

"Thank you Dr. Burnim. I'm very proud of these young men. They worked hard throughout the season and peaked at the right time. They deserve it."

"This is your first CIAA championship as a coach. How does it feel?"

"It's unbelievable! It's hard to put into words. Leading my alma mater to the championship! I feel really blessed!"

This tournament championship is one of the joys of leadership.—putting the right people into the right place and giving them the chance to succeed. When I approved the hiring of Coach Brooks, I helped put him in a position to succeed. When he hired assistant coaches and recruited student athletes, he put them into a position to succeed. One major role of a leader is to empower others to grow and succeed!

THE COMMENCEMENT VENUE

During the 2011-12 academic year, the university's Commencement Committee invited me to one of their meetings where they presented me with a recommendation. They met in the third-floor conference room of the administration building and, as I recall, Cynthia Coleman, chair of the Staff Council, convened the meeting and spoke for the committee.

"Dr. Burnim," she said, "In order to mitigate several problems stemming from holding our spring commencement exercises in the campus football stadium, we recommend holding the spring 2013 commencement in the Comcast Center on the University of Maryland College Park campus. Because this would be a big departure from our campus tradition, we recommend that you announce the move a year in advance to give the campus community ample time to make the mental adjustment to this change."

"Thank you, Ms. Coleman and the committee," I said. "I applaud the initiative you've shown in not just planning for this year's commencement but also taking a longer range view and thinking about what will best accommodate our needs for the future. What specifically led you to make this recommendation?"

"Dr. Burnim, there are several problems that we have to contend with every year when we hold commencement on campus. First, the crowd is so large that the campus can't accommodate all the vehicles that need to park. Hence, people are forced to park along Highway 197 and that's dangerous. Second, because we need to be prepared for unpredictable weather conditions, our staff must set up indoor space in addition to setting up the football field. And if we're forced to go inside, then the number of guests who can attend for each graduate has to be reduced to no more than four. Third, there's the general discomfort of holding it outdoors in May. It gets hot sitting in the sun about an hour into the two-hours-long event and we have had people passing out."

"You make a very strong case. I'll share the plan with our campus constituencies and we'll prepare to go to the Comcast Center in 2013." I felt good about moving forward with the committee's recommendation because it was composed of students and representatives from the shared governance groups—the Faculty Senate, the Staff Council, the

Student Government Association, and the Graduate Student Association and they all supported the recommendation. Plus we were going to give people a year to get used to the idea. What could possibly go wrong with that?

Over the course of the next year, I met with faculty, staff, students, and alumni sharing the recommendation and seeking their input. In December 2012, I called a general faculty meeting where I gave a PowerPoint presentation to update them on a number of things happening on the campus. At the end of my presentation, I made an announcement: "I think all of you are aware that last year the Commencement Committee recommended that we hold our 2013 spring commencement in the Comcast Center at UM College Park, which would allow as many family members and friends of the graduates who desired to attend to do so, to park safely, and enjoy the ceremony in air conditioned comfort. I've spent the last several months discussing it with faculty, staff, students, and alumni trying to gauge the will of the majority. Having done so, I am announcing today that our 2013 spring commencement will be in the Comcast Center.

As I recall, James Jones immediately blurted out, "What? We don't want to go to Maryland University! They wouldn't let me go to college there when I finished high school and I don't want to have anything to do with them! This is a bad decision! I'm changing next week's Faculty Senate meeting to a Faculty Association meeting!"

This last comment embodied the threat of another "no confidence" vote.

The loudest and most persistent objections came from a handful of faculty and alumni—apparently led by Jones and Sarah Bullock, respectively. To get a better reading of what constituents thought, I commissioned a survey of faculty, staff, and students. It revealed that majorities of all three groups supported the move. In fact, student support for it was overwhelming. The principal objection raised by Jones and Bullock was that, when they were youth, the University of Maryland College Park would not admit them as students due to its racism. Hence, they strongly objected to having the BSU commencement on that campus. I certainly didn't deny the racist history of UM College Park but thought that the good that would come from our commencement guests having safe places to park and being able to enjoy the ceremony in air-conditioned comfort provided much greater benefit than would a protest/boycott of the University of Maryland College Park for wrongs long ago committed.

No matter how their objections were responded to or how the reasons for the decision were explained, or the fact that students, for whom the commencement ceremony was being held, supported it, the opponents continued to object and try different tactics to reverse the decision.

Upon the strong advice of my cabinet, I decided to attend the Faculty Association meeting. It was held in a tiered lecture hall in the Martin Luther King Jr. Building with an estimated capacity of about eighty people. Altogether, about fifty people were seated on the various levels, including eight or ten alumni, with Bullock being among them. I surmised that they had been specifically invited because alumni, staff, and students don't normally attend meetings of the general faculty. As I recall, no students were present, so I figured that either students weren't invited, or they chose not to accept invitations.

Jones stood at the front of the room on the lowest level. I sat at a table about midway up the tiers of seats and to his right. My cabinet members sat near me, and most of the faculty members and alumni sat in seats on the various tiers to his left.

He called the meeting to order and then ranted and raved for fifteen or twenty minutes. His diatribe sounded something like this: "When the president announced at the Town Hall meeting that he was moving the graduation to the Comcast Center, I decided then that we need to change the scheduled Faculty Senate meeting to a Faculty Association meeting because we might need to take a vote! When I graduated from high school, Maryland University discriminated against me and wouldn't let me or anyone who looked like me enroll there! They didn't want us there then, so why should we go over there now? I think maybe they're having trouble paying for the Comcast Center and the president agreed to help them out by paying to rent it."

I felt like a volcano of anger was about to erupt from inside me, and would not have been surprised if steam had been coming out of my ears! This was demagoguery at its best! As he talked, he mostly looked down toward the floor or the table in front of him, occasionally lifting his head to glance around. Was this a sign that he felt a tinge of shame for what he was doing?

When he had finished, he called for a vote on the move to the Comcast Center by secret ballot. He tallied the ballots and announced: "ten for; thirty-four against." Jones then looked up toward me and asked, "President—do you want to say anything?"

As I responded, "Yes, I do," I prayed silently: *Lord, give me strength. Help me to love my enemies as you command, and glorify you.* "Thank you, Dr. Jones," I said calmly as I stood and walked down a couple of tiers toward him. "First, I forgive you for what you have just done and want you to know that I love you and there's nothing you can do about it!" He started to respond, then caught himself. I turned my back to him and faced the faculty and alumni on the left side of the room. "It's interesting that we find ourselves at this point. Over the course of the last year, I thought that I had taken all of the right steps—sharing with students, faculty, staff, and alumni the recommendation from the committee, weighing comments and reactions and, finally, making a decision that was heavily favored by the graduating students who are the intended beneficiaries of the commencement exercises. And yet we find ourselves at this point." I paused for a moment to let that sink in and then continued. "I hear your objections and appreciate the intensity of your feelings about this. I haven't signed a contract to use the Comcast Center, so maybe I need to reconsider. I'll mull this over, but have to leave now to go to a rehearsal for our winter commencement tomorrow." A faculty member told me later that after I left the meeting, Dr. Jones tried to call for a vote of "no confidence," but some of the senior faculty quashed it.

I had survived that attack, but others were to follow. After that meeting, I did reconsider the decision to move the commencement ceremony. While doing so, I received encouragement from a few people around the campus. One staff member asked Ward to tell me to listen to a specific sermon by Charles Stanley, and I did. In addition to absorbing these encouraging messages, I turned to biblical scripture and prayer. I was reminded that God's sovereignty rules over everything and that "All things work together for good for those who love the Lord and are called according to his purpose." The battle is not mine, it's the Lord's. My job is not to fight, but to stand!

Thank you, Lord, for giving me clarity on how I should proceed with regard to this spring commencement issue! I wrote in my journal. Though I was confident that I had already accurately assessed the true sentiment of the vast majority of our campus constituencies, I decided to administer a survey of faculty, staff, and students regarding the question, which I expected would reflect their support and maybe convince the very vocal and active opponents.

While I was dealing with this issue on the campus, my family and I were also dealing with a personal crisis. My son's son, Akim, a two-year old, had been diagnosed with a rare form of cancer, which was threatening to take his life. Throughout the ordeal, he spent a total of six months in Children's National Hospital, four of which were in the Intensive Care Unit! This meant that for portions of each day my mind was taken off my work challenges, but my stress level didn't change because it was just trading focus from one stressor to another.

Meanwhile, the attacks and challenges continued. In a University Council meeting in February, Jones questioned: "Where did you get the funds to install lights on the football field? And aren't there more important things to spend the money on? How did you decide to spend it on the lights?" It was as if he was now going out of his way to find things to criticize and argue about. During some of our conversations, Jones talked about how he had been mistreated by previous presidents. I was told that he had been removed from the head football coach position many years earlier, and wondered if his anger emanated, in part, from those perceived injustices.

"Dr. Jones, when you have a question about something, you can come to me directly and ask. You don't have to try to trap me by springing things on me in an open meeting like this. We try to be completely transparent and open."

"It just came up," he said. "Where did the money come from?"

"The money came through a special appropriation from the general assembly. It was specifically for the lights on the football field so it could not have been spent on anything else." I sensed that he came very close to accusing me of lying, but stopped short of doing so.

"I'll find out," he mumbled. And that was the last time he ever mentioned the matter.

Later that same month, I received mean-spirited letters from two alumni who were upset about my decision to move the commencement.

During this period, Akim began a new chemotherapy protocol. It was very difficult for him and, therefore, for his parents and grandparents as well.

One day around the first of March, I buzzed Ward on the intercom. "Mrs. Ward: please call Dr. Jones and invite him to have lunch with me at my expense. He can pick the restaurant. Maybe we can come to a meeting of the minds over a goodwill lunch."

A little while later, she walked into my office. "I spoke to Dr. Jones and extended your invitation. He declined without explanation."

"Thanks, Mrs. Ward."

I heard later that some faculty were planning a protest or demonstration for the Board of Regents meeting in Baltimore. That was to be followed by a second protest/demonstration at the USM System office in Adelphi, and then another vote of "no confidence" in the president at the April Faculty Association meeting. In addition, some members of the Maryland General Assembly were asking questions about the commencement noise they were hearing, so someone had approached them about the matter. I saw all of this as part of an escalation strategy, and was pleased that neither of the rumored protests took place. As a precautionary measure, I did write a letter to some members of the assembly explaining what was going on.

The Faculty Association meeting was held and, given his position as chair of the Faculty Senate, Jones presided. As he called the meeting to order, he seemed to have a singular objective in mind. I recall that he challenged the small group in attendance with a series of questions: "Do you support me or not?" he asked. "Ya'll came to me and asked me to lead and I agreed to do so. Do I have your support?" Then he said, "I make the motion of support for me. Can I get a second?" After an awkward moment of silence, he repeated himself. "Can I get a second for my motion?" The room was quiet enough to hear a proverbial pin drop as Jones looked around the room for someone to second his motion. When no one did, he mumbled, "Well, ya'll can have it," and he started gathering his belongings from the desk in front of him. When he had picked them all up, he tucked them under his arm, announced "I quit," and walked out of the meeting.

In April, I heard a rumor that Jones was trying to organize a faculty boycott of commencement. Escalation! Increasing the pressure by generating negative publicity seemed to be the strategy. And then we got the news!

"President Burnim! President Burnim!" my chief of staff called to me as she rushed into my office. "Michelle Obama has accepted our invitation to be the speaker for our May commencement!"

A broad smile spread across my face immediately. Months earlier we had gone through the official channels to invite the First Lady of the United States (FLOTUS) to keynote our May 17, 2013 commencement. We were told that she and her staff would consider it but would not notify us of her decision until a few weeks prior to the ceremony. We were hopeful, but figured that the odds were against us. Everybody wanted the First Lady! So her coming to Bowie State was a big deal for us!

"Tammi, that's great news! And it couldn't have come at a better time!"

It meant that our commencement would attract national media attention and a lot of people who had never heard of Bowie State would learn something about it! I was excited because that kind of attention could have a positive impact on our admissions applications and fundraising. Also, I was pretty sure that the excitement around the campus about her coming would dampen the noise surrounding the venue change and support for a boycott. In addition to all of that, we received word that my grandson's new protocol was taking hold and he was now making great progress! In fact, he would be well enough to go home soon. God is good!

On the day of the commencement, LaVera and I left home earlier than usual to arrive at the Comcast Center well before the scheduled time for the ceremony. It was a sunny day and even as we drove to College Park I was already starting to feel the joy that always accompanied commencement. What was usually a special day was even more special this time because Michelle Obama would be our featured speaker and this would make Bowie State the envy of many colleges and universities across the country!

Security at the center was tight because of FLOTUS so we stopped at the checkpoint so they could verify our names on the list of people who were to be admitted to the area where Obama would be before the ceremony began. Since the opportunity to meet her was such a rare privilege, I invited my daughter, granddaughter, son, and sister Mellonee to be our guests, and we rendezvoused with them in the holding room to await our chance to meet her. As her caravan neared the Comcast Center, the First Lady's advance team ushered us to the area where we would meet her and take a picture with her. I was already in my gold-colored academic gown with four black stripes on each arm, which indicated my leadership position. LaVera wore a black skirt and a colorful patterned sleeveless blouse. Cinnamon, Madison, Mellonee, and Adrian were all decked out in their Sunday best.

The First Lady walked into the meeting area and one of her public relations staffers immediately positioned her in front of the photo backdrop equidistant between the US and Maryland flags. Another one of her staffers then introduced us to her by reading our names from a list as we greeted her and shook her hand.

"Dr. Mickey L. Burnim, President of Bowie State University."

"Thank you for accepting our invitation," I told her. "We look forward to hearing your address!"

"Mrs. LaVera Burnim, First Lady of Bowie State University."

"Hello, First Lady!" LaVera said. "We're thrilled to meet you! Thank you for coming." LaVera extended her arms to embrace the First Lady. True to her reputation as a genuine and humble person, Obama reached out to embrace LaVera as she commented, "More tall women!" She was specifically referring to LaVera, who is almost six feet tall, and our daughter, Cinnamon, who is six feet tall. LaVera stood on one side of her and I stood on the other and the rest of the family filled in as we posed for her photographer and captured this very special moment!

The ceremony itself came off without a hitch. Early in the program, I conferred The Presidential Medal of Excellence on Dr. Freeman Hrabowski, the inimitable president of the University of Maryland Baltimore County, who weeks earlier had agreed to be our backup keynote speaker in case something unexpected caused FLOTUS to cancel.

I thought FLOTUS's address was the best out of the scores I had heard over the years! She was warm and engaging and spoke with great passion about the importance of getting an education: "Today getting an education is as important if not more important than it was back when this university was founded . . . no matter what career you pursue, every single one of you has a role to play as educators for our young people."

Obama got the loudest applause when she highlighted a couple of the graduates and their struggles and sacrifices to reach this point. Urging the graduates to show grit and determination, like those who founded BSU back in 1865, she referred to Ariel Williams Edwards, a member of the graduating class who has shown that same kind of grit and determination:

"Ariel's mother struggled with substance abuse and Ariel and her sister were removed from her care and sent to live with their grandmother. But Ariel decided to draw inspiration from her struggle. She majored in social work so she could help families like hers."

The graduates appreciated Obama's vicarious recognition of each of them by singling out one of them. As she spoke, her eyes barely paused on the teleprompter in front of the podium as they moved across the audience like a butterfly fluttering from one irresistible flower to another and then another. The wrinkles in her brow conveyed the heartfelt seriousness with which she spoke.

She then personalized her message and wrapped it up. "And there is not a day that goes by when I don't think about the sacrifices my mom and dad made for me . . . now it is up to all of you to carry that legacy forward, to be that flame of faith, that torch of truth to guide our young people toward a better future for themselves and this country."

After she finished, I thanked her on behalf of the assemblage.

"First Lady Obama," I said, "thank you very much for that wonderful history lesson, for that insightful reality check, and for that inspirational and sincere message. By your presence today you have made this already wonderful day and occasion of celebration even more special. We will always remember it and we will always carry love for you and for the President and your family in our hearts. Thank you! And God bless you!"

It was a wonderful day and our first commencement in the Comcast Center had been a rousing success!

Service under Grace

The mountain-top experience of the May 2013 commencement lasted a couple of weeks before we had to sharpen our focus on goals, objectives, and priorities for the next year. The new fiscal year would begin on July 1 and, once again, I needed the campus leaders to be clear about our priorities as we approached it. Improving the university's graduation rates, identifying and emphasizing signature programs, and enhancing our funding stream were at the top of the list, and part of my job was to remind members of the campus community and our supporters just how we would go about accomplishing those things: How would we admit and graduate more students? How would we convince legislators in the Maryland General Assembly that we really needed the additional $15 million for the new science building? We had to refine our messages for donors, legislators, students, alumni and supporters, and hone our communication strategies.

Our time, energy, and attention for these tasks, however, had to be split with that needed for dealing with the continuing opposition that grew out of the commencement venue decision. Even after Jones' resignation, I still had to deal with attacks on my leadership. Dr. Rebecca Waterford succeeded Jones as chair of the Faculty Senate and she seemed bent on maintaining the same kind of acrimonious relationship with the university's administration as he had fostered. At one point, she notified then USM Chancellor Robert Caret that the faculty had taken a "no confidence" vote against Provost Jackson and stated their reasons for doing so. On its face, this was an attack on the provost. But given all of the history leading to the hiring of this provost, it would have been very dangerous for me to leave this attack unchallenged.

I saw those reasons as being without merit and wrote a response to her, which I copied to Chancellor Caret. I addressed each of the points in her complaint and concluded with the following:

> After reading carefully your explanation for the "no confidence" vote in Provost Jackson and responding to each area, my impression of Provost Jackson's performance remains positive. . . . He works hard, brings a wealth of experience from other higher education institutions to the job, is collegial and committed to shared governance, and I believe that he operates with great integrity . . . I note, however, that none of us is perfect and we all have room for improvement. I will continue to work with Provost Jackson, and with all of my direct reports, to help them to grow professionally and improve their overall job performance.
>
> Finally, I must comment about the process used to raise these issues. As I said to you during a recent meeting, the forwarding of grievances, concerns, and internal issues to people and organizations outside the university before they have been raised and discussed appropriately internally does unnecessary harm to the university's public image. This negativity makes student, staff, and faculty recruitment more difficult, as well as fundraising and continuing support from other important constituencies, like the Maryland general assembly. . . . The approach of taking votes of "no confidence" and sending a list of grievances to the newspapers or the Chancellor before making a good-faith attempt to resolve them on campus reinforces the impression throughout the region of Bowie State being a bastion of continuous internal bickering with a total lack of cohesion, and of it being an unpleasant place to work and study.
>
> I sincerely hope that we . . . will grow to the point where we can have open and honest discussions about matters

of real importance and disagree, when we must, without being disagreeable, and accept that not every decision will be made so that everyone is satisfied. . . . We should discuss matters of importance collegially and in good faith and try to arrive at the best approaches and solutions for the total university. . . . We should also understand and accept that, in the final analysis, the President is held responsible by the Chancellor and Board of Regents for the well-being and operation of the university, and that his decisions made directly or through delegated officers are the official positions for the university. Let's work together for the uplifting of Bowie State University with laser-like focus on growing our enrollment and improving our graduation rate!

In addition, alumni opponents also persisted in their campaign to have the commencement venue decision reversed. At a November alumni meeting six months after our first use of the Comcast Center, for example, Sarah Bullock presented me with a package of petitions signed by people opposing the Comcast Center.

This opposition persisted for most of the next four years, but we stuck with the decision and held each spring commencement in the Comcast Center through 2017, my last one before retirement. Many people appreciated the move and enjoyed the advantages that it offered—relief from sitting directly in the sun, ample, convenient, and safe parking, and air conditioning. They were just not as vocal in their support.

I also received words of encouragement from numerous people during this period. My wife, LaVera, was a stalwart for me. On those days when I didn't want to burden her with the attacks on my leadership, she would read my body language and ask, "What's wrong?" or "What happened today?" She would then listen patiently as I told the story, then say, "Well, you're doing an excellent job!" Or, "We expected this!

We knew that Bowie State had a culture of fighting their presidents and administrations that goes back twenty years!"

There were also timely handwritten notes or email messages from faculty and staff members on the campus. I received prayers, prophecies, encouragement, and expressions of appreciation from Ward, Dr. Nwokeafor, Edna Palmer, Dr. Sammye Miller, Minister Janice Bennett, Reverend Joy, Sharon Person, Adrian Burnim, Cinnamon Bowser, and others. These expressions fortified my spirit and helped me to keep moving forward to see what the end would be. I experienced firsthand the power of an encouraging word at the right time!

It was also during this period that I received one of the highest honors of my higher education career. I was invited to give the "President to Presidents Lecture" at the annual meeting of the American Association of State Colleges and Universities (AASCU). AASCU is the national organization of presidents and chancellors who lead its nearly 400-member institutions, ranging in enrollment from about 1,000 students to more than 45,000. LaVera and I had been active in the organization for twenty years attending its annual and summer meetings, serving on committees, and participating in its programs. I was even elected to serve as chair of the AASCU Board on two different occasions. Nevertheless, I was surprised and deeply honored when I received the letter from AASCU President Dr. Muriel Howard, notifying me that the board had selected me to give the lecture at the 2016 annual meeting. *Wow!* I thought. *I didn't realize that the member presidents and chancellors thought so well of me. This is really special!*

I had come to view every opportunity to speak before an audience as a privilege that should be appreciated and not squandered. Hence, I chose to encourage and challenge my presidential colleagues.

I titled my lecture, "The Challenge of Presidential Leadership," and posed a question: "What does our society need and how can AASCU Presidents lead so as to provide it? . . . The challenge that I want to focus on for a few minutes today, however, is one of very longstanding and seeming intractability. And that is the issue of race. At the turn of the twentieth century, W. E. B. DuBois wrote, 'The problem of the twentieth century is the problem of the color line.' Most of you here today are old enough to remember the turbulent 1960s and know from those memories that DuBois had certainly been right. Sadly, I submit that the problem of the color line is still very much with us in the twenty-first century! The evidence is all around us."

The setting for the program was a luncheon, and the room was set up with round tables seating about ten people each. From my position at the lectern on the elevated stage at the front of the room, I scanned the room as I spoke, trying to make eye contact with my audience, as a good speaker should. More than that, however, I was looking for LaVera to get some visual feedback. Whenever she happened to be in my audience, I had learned to look at her face. If it showed a quizzical look, I knew that I was being unclear. If she raised her hand slightly from the table and made an up and down motion, I knew that I needed to slow my speaking pace.

LaVera was pretty widely recognized for her good judgment and common sense—throughout the family and among people who knew her. Our daughter, Cinnamon, and her husband, Steve, asked for her counsel and advice before buying a house. "Mom," Cinnamon asked, "should we buy this house in Alexandria even though it would need some remodeling?"

After visiting the house and being told its listing price, LaVera advised, "Cinnamon, you and Steve ought to look at some neighborhoods a little farther out. You would still be in northern Virginia but could get a lot more house for your money."

Once, Adrian, our son, called seeking some specific guidance: "Mom, I want to start my own business for serving youth who need help in learning how to be hopeful, make plans for the future, and manage their anger. There's such a great need and I believe this would be a great time. What do you think?"

"Adrian, I think you ought to go ahead and become fully certified as a clinical social worker first," she advised. "That would give you greater credibility and incentive for government agencies to send business your way!"

Today, her face showed a calm slight smile. That, and the rapt attention of the rest of the audience, told me that I had gotten off to a good start!

My practice paid off and the speech went very well. I was gratified when, at the end, my colleagues and their guests gave me a standing ovation! Several of them came up to congratulate me and shake my hand. President Howard told me, "Mickey, you have raised the bar for the 'President to Presidents Lecture'!"

My final year at Bowie State involved a good bit of reflection and celebration. I announced my retirement at the university's fall convocation in 2016. Traditionally, it was our first convocation of each academic year. The faculty donned their academic regalia and marched in to occupy the middle rows of the Meyers Auditorium in the Martin Luther King Jr. Building. Students—largely student government officers, other elected leaders, and student athletes—filled the rows across the aisle to the right of the faculty. The university's gospel choir sang, the Student Government officers were sworn into their elected offices for the year, and I gave the keynote address. As we neared the end of the program, from my seat on the stage with the other program participants, I went back to the podium to make my announcement:

> I mentioned earlier that this fall marked fifty years since I was a college freshman. That makes this fall the fiftieth anniversary of my involvement in higher education. It has been a tremendous journey of service through my teaching and leading. It has been my pleasure to teach both undergraduates and graduate students, and even guide PhD candidates on dissertation committees. I have also enjoyed serving the higher education community through the regional accreditation process and national presidential associations, as well as providing leadership as a university system official, provost, chancellor, and president. Clearly, God has shown me extraordinary favor!

After that opening, I continued by recounting some of the things we had accomplished over the last ten years including increased graduation numbers, national rankings, new degree programs and buildings, and an enhanced reputation. And then I told them:

> As Bowie State continues its rise to becoming the best comprehensive university in the nation, the time has come for me to transition to spending more time enjoying my family and serving the higher education and broader communities in more focused and limited ways. In preparation for this shift in focus, I have notified Chancellor Caret of my intention to retire from the presidency of Bowie State University effective June 30, 2017.

Immediately, the auditorium erupted in spontaneous and sustained applause. It seemed that the entire assembly of faculty, students, and staff rose to their feet and clapped for several minutes. *Oh my!* I thought. *They really have appreciated my leadership!* I had not worked to gain approval or recognition, but rather to advance the mission of the university in the "right" way. But I soaked up the applause and was thankful! At that moment, I felt validation from the vast majority of the faculty for what we had accomplished and how I had led—representing and advocating for the university, operating with integrity and transparency, and maintaining persistent focus on what was most important for the university. I felt very grateful for the strength, vision, and courage God had given me to lead Bowie State University!

Moving Forward

Effective leadership, that which makes a difference, depends upon good relationships with people, i.e. those who would follow. It must be all about working for the benefit of others in ways that they find acceptable. This means taking account of their values and culture. Good relationships with people are based on trust, which is built through integrity. Integrity is the combination of truthfulness and reliability.

Leaders need to understand that, at some point, they will be criticized and face opposition. The truth of this can be seen in the experiences of the earliest leaders in the Bible to those of current day US Presidents and other world leaders. Sometimes those who would be followers can't see around corners or as far ahead as the leader. At other times, well-meaning people simply disagree. In any case, the leader may have to proceed to do the "right thing" even though he/she may have to face negative consequences, such as votes of "no confidence," losing elections, or even greater losses. The leader's ultimate concern must always be to maximize the benefit to those affected by the leadership!

As I contemplated retiring from active leadership, I looked around for ways to remain active and productive. I remembered my introduction to executive coaching while serving as chancellor for ECSU and thought this would be a good way to continue to contribute to good leadership by using my experience and skills, but at a pace more suited to this stage of my life. Hence, I began a process that led to my becoming a certified executive coach through the International Coaching Federation. I now serve actual and aspirational leaders through coaching and consulting. Positions of leadership are often lonely and almost always complex. Having a coach or consultant to partner with can be an invaluable resource.

If you are seeking ways to become a more effective leader, I invite you to contact me at Burnim Leadership Development and Coaching about a potential partnership.

NOTES

1. *The Teague Chronicle*, August 19, 1965, vol 50, no. 9.
2. James L. Rogers, *The Story of North Texas: From Texas Normal College, 1890, to the University of North Texas System, 2001*, (Denton: University of North Texas Press, 2002), 353.
3. Jim Collins, *Good to Great* (New York: Harper Business, 2001).
4. John Maxwell, *The 21 Irrefutable Laws of Leadership* (Nashville: Thomas Nelson Publishers, 1998).
5. Noel M. Tichy, *The Leadership Engine* (New York: Harper Business, 1997).
6. Tichy, *The Leadership Engine*, 44-45.
7. Tichy, *The Leadership Engine*, 50.
8. "Maryland's Report and the Partnership Agreement Between the State of Maryland and the U. S. Department of Education, Office for Civil Rights" Maryland Higher Education Commission, accessed September 23, 2023, mhec.maryland.gov/Pages/ocrplan.aspx.
9. "Tim Newman exits Charlotte Regional Visitors Authority," *Charlotte Business Journal*, February 24, 2012, https://www.bizjournals.com/charlotte/news/2012/02/24/tim-newman-exits-charlotte-regional.html.

www.ingramcontent.com/pod-product-compliance
Lightning Source LLC
Chambersburg PA
CBHW070647160426
43194CB00009B/1620